Every Decker book is accompanied by a CD-ROM.

The disc appears in the front of each copy, in its own sealed jacket. Affixed to the front of the book will be a distinctive BcD sticker **"Book *cum* disc."**

The disc contains the complete text and illustrations of the book, in fully searchable PDF files. The book and disc are sold *only* as a package; neither is available independently, and no prices are available for the items individually.

BC Decker Inc is committed to providing high-quality electronic publications that complement traditional information and learning methods.

We trust you will find the book/CD package invaluable and invite your comments and suggestions.

Brian C. Decker
CEO and Publisher

CONQUERING
HEADACHE

FOURTH EDITION

An Illustrated Guide to Understanding
the Treatment and Control of Headache

ALAN M. RAPOPORT, MD
FRED D. SHEFTELL, MD
STEWART J. TEPPER, MD

2003
Decker DTC
Hamilton • London

Decker DTC
An Imprint of BC Decker Inc
20 Hughson Street South
P.O. Box 620, LCD 1
Hamilton, Ontario L8N 3K7
Tel: 905-522-7017; 800-568-7281
Fax: 905-522-7839; 888-311-4987
E-mail: info@bcdecker.com
www.bcdecker.com

03 04 05 06/GSA/9 8 7 6 5 4 3 2 1

ISBN 1-55009-233-2
Printed in Spain

Sales and Distribution

United States
BC Decker Inc
P.O. Box 785
Lewiston, NY 14092-0785
Tel: 905-522-7017; 800-568-7281
Fax: 905-522-7839; 888-311-4987
E-mail: info@bcdecker.com
www.bcdecker.com

Canada
BC Decker Inc
20 Hughson Street South
P.O. Box 620, LCD 1
Hamilton, Ontario L8N 3K7
Tel: 905-522-7017; 800-568-7281
Fax: 905-522-7839; 888-311-4987
E-mail: info@bcdecker.com
www.bcdecker.com

Foreign Rights
John Scott & Company
International Publishers' Agency
P.O. Box 878
Kimberton, PA 19442
Tel: 610-827-1640
Fax: 610-827-1671
E-mail: jsco@voicenet.com

Japan
Igaku-Shoin Ltd.
Foreign Publications Department
3-24-17 Hongo
Bunkyo-ku, Tokyo, Japan 113-8719
Tel: 3 3817 5680
Fax: 3 3815 6776
E-mail: fd@igaku-shoin.co.jp

*U.K., Europe, Scandinavia,
Middle East*
Elsevier Science
Customer Service Department
Foots Cray High Street
Sidcup, Kent
DA14 5HP, UK
Tel: 44 (0) 208 308 5760
Fax: 44 (0) 181 308 5702
E-mail: cservice@harcourt.com

*Singapore, Malaysia, Thailand,
Philippines, Indonesia, Vietnam,
Pacific Rim, Korea*
Elsevier Science Asia
583 Orchard Road
#09/01, Forum
Singapore 238884
Tel: 65-737-3593
Fax: 65-753-2145

Australia, New Zealand
Elsevier Science Australia
Customer Service Department
STM Division
Locked Bag 16
St. Peters, New South Wales, 2044
Australia
Tel: 61 02 9517-8999
Fax: 61 02 9517-2249
E-mail: stmp@harcourt.com.au
www.harcourt.com.au

Mexico and Central America
ETM SA de CV
Calle de Tula 59
Colonia Condesa
06140 Mexico DF, Mexico
Tel: 52-5-5553-6657
Fax: 52-5-5211-8468
E-mail:editoresdetextosmex@
prodigy.net.mx

Argentina
CLM (Cuspide Libros Medicos)
Av. Córdoba 2067 - (1120)
Buenos Aires, Argentina
Tel: (5411) 4961-0042/
(5411) 4964-0848
Fax: (5411) 4963-7988
E-mail: clm@cuspide.com

Brazil
Tecmedd
Av. Maurílio Biagi, 2850
City Ribeirão Preto – SP – CEP:
14021-000
Tel: 0800 992236
Fax: (16) 3993-9000

ACKNOWLEDGMENTS

We gratefully acknowledge Adrienne Harkavy for her fine touch in editing many drafts of our manuscript. We thank Stephen Mader for his excellent illustrations. A special acknowledgement to Starr Pearlman for her help with the MIDAS section and to Alice Batenhorst for her help with the HIT section.

DEDICATIONS

To our patients who have taught us so much. Don't give up hope.

In loving memory of my father, Joe Sheftell.

Fred

To Abigail Rose Rapoport, my beautiful first grandchild, and to all the next generation of Rapoports that we hope to welcome in the future.

Alan

To my wife, Deb, and my sons, Clinton and Sam. Your help and love inspire me continually. To my parents, Clifford and Cynthia.

Stew

The first edition of *Conquering Headache* was published in 1995; since that time our understanding of headache has vastly improved and a variety of new treatments have become available or are about to emerge. We wrote this fourth edition to keep our readers up to date as new developments change the way we think about and treat headache.

Each year over 45 million people in the United States seek medical attention for head pain. Over 12% (30 million) of our population have migraine, often disabling them. Though headache is an illness largely misunderstood, misdiagnosed, and mistreated, consultation rates have tripled and recognition rates have increased in the past decade. The overwhelming majority of headaches are not life threatening, yet they can be painful and debilitating. For too many, headache disrupts daily routines and impairs quality of life.

The vast majority of people with frequent headaches do not have brain tumors, aneurysms (weaknesses in the walls of the blood vessels within the head), allergies, sinus infections, or significant dental problems. The most common types of headache are migraine, tension-type headache, and, to a much lesser extent, cluster headache. These three "primary" headaches are not caused by other medical conditions, nor are they caused by psychological factors. Rather, the primary headaches are the result of biologic mechanisms in the brain, nerves, blood vessels, and muscles. Can emotional factors play a role? Of course they can; but mostly they act as headache triggers or modulators, not causes.

This book reveals the truth about headache and dispels many common myths. These are the bare facts:

- Headache is not imagined.
- Allergies are not a frequent cause of headache.
- Most headaches are not due to sinus problems.

- Most headache sufferers do not have significant temporomandibular joint syndrome.
- More medication taken for headache is not better treatment. In many cases less medication taken, optimally and early, may offer more relief.

The bottom line about headaches is that you do not have to learn to live with them! In this book we provide you with the information you need to conquer your headaches and improve the quality of your life. You will find the latest information about treatment with medication as well as state-of-the-art updates on nutrition, exercise, sleep habits, behavioral techniques, and pain management. You also will find information about massage, physical therapy, and alternative therapies including chiropractic, acupuncture, and natural remedies such as vitamins, minerals, and herbs.

In addition, we give you practical guidelines for medication use—dosages, side effects, and limitations on its use—as well as the tools you need to get your headaches under control and to monitor your progress on paper. The record-keeping system that we describe in this book is the same one we give to patients in our practice. It includes our original headache calendar to monitor your headache progress, medication intake and effectiveness, level of disability, and headache triggers, and—for women—menstrual cycles and hormone replacement therapy.

This fourth edition of *Conquering Headache* gives you clear guidelines for dealing with headache in the workplace and school, for understanding the impact of migraine on the individual and society, and for using disability rating scales to aid in communicating with your doctor. Suggestions are provided for children, parents, and teachers. This book should not be used to self-diagnose or self-treat. We encourage you to learn all you can about headache and to work closely with your doctor to gain control over your headache problem.

Remember, you are in charge. The most important factor in conquering your headache is your willingness to take responsibility, which means you must take an active role in your own recovery. This book alone cannot do it for you, and your doctor cannot do it for you. However, this book does offer information and guidelines to enable you to learn to control your headache rather than let it control you. Good luck!

Alan Rapoport, MD
Fred Sheftell, MD
Stewart Tepper, MD

CONTENTS

CHAPTER 1

HISTORY OF HEADACHE

The experience of headache has been around as long as the human race. Our ancestors believed that headache was visited upon us as punishment for offending the gods or that it occurred when humans became possessed by evil spirits. Through the ages treatment has been directed at the suspected cause; not surprisingly, headache remedies were aimed at ridding the body of demons. Thus, the earliest neurosurgeons bored holes in the skull through which the

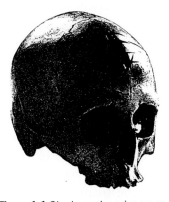

Figure 1-1 Slash marks crisscross a gaping hole in a twelfth or thirteenth century Peruvian girl's skull. The hole shows no signs of bone regrowth, so the girl likely died as a result of her operation. (From the National Museum of Natural History, Washington, DC, catalogue #178473)

headache-causing demons could escape. Skulls with evidence of such surgery (called *trephination*) have been found in Peru and date back to the thirteenth century (Figure 1-1).

Hippocrates, a physician who practiced in ancient Greece, noticed that vomiting ended some attacks of head pain, so he prescribed herbs to cause it. He also used another treatment—the application of leeches or bloodletting through small cuts, a practice that persisted through the Middle Ages. The ancient Egyptians wrapped the heads of sufferers in linen along with a clay crocodile holding in its mouth wheat from the gods' storehouse (Figure 1-2).

In the seventeenth century, Thomas Willis theorized that headache pain was related to swollen blood vessels in the head. Erasmus Darwin, Charles Darwin's grandfather, further explored these theories. Interestingly, both Charles and Erasmus Darwin suffered from migraine headache.

In the late nineteenth century, an English neurologist named Liveing was the first doctor to write that headaches, similar to seizures, were "nerve storms," affecting the nerves of the head more than the blood vessels.

Folk remedies such as tying rags around the head or applying tobacco stamps to the head had their advocates, as do herbal remedies still. Heat, cold, acupuncture, chiropractic manipulation, nerve blocks, diets, laser therapies, hyperbaric oxygen, and hysterectomies have also been proposed as headache treatments. There is no shortage of conflicting opinion and information, adding to headache sufferers' confusion about which treatments may help.

It is generally not possible to completely cure your headache. What you can expect is fewer headaches and better control of the pain. The remainder of this book tells you how to take control of your headaches.

Figure 1-2 Egyptian with clay crocodile with herbs in its mouth placed on his head for headache treatment. (Courtesy of John Edmeads, MD)

CHAPTER 2

IMPACT OF HEADACHE ON SOCIETY

More patients who visit doctors complain of headache than of any other single ailment. Yet migraine—and headache in general—continues to be underdiagnosed, misdiagnosed, and mistreated. Recent studies show that more than half of migraineurs have not been diagnosed with migraine by a physician. If patients do not have the diagnosis of migraine, they will not get the proper treatment for it. Although medical students and even neurology residents in the hospital learn a great deal about serious causes of headache, such as tumors, strokes, aneurysms, and meningitis, they do not learn much about migraine and tension-type headache, the types they will see most frequently in their offices.

In the past several years, some off-the-shelf pain relievers have been approved by the United States Food and Drug Administration as effective for migraine or "migraine pain" and have been allowed to advertise on television and in newspapers and magazines. These medications, such as Excedrin Migraine, Advil Migraine, and Motrin Migraine Pain, can be effective when used infrequently for mild attacks. However, since they are available without prescription, the manufacturers do not have to provide a safety warning in the ads, even though the medications can cause major problems. We warn our patients taking off-the-shelf painkillers to be aware of gastrointestinal symptoms, heartburn, stomach ulcers, long-term liver or kidney problems, easy bruisability, and the development of daily headache (*analgesic rebound headache*, also called *chronic migraine with medication overuse*).

Headaches may occasionally be due to allergies or sinus problems, but the majority of patients with allergies do not usually get headaches from them. Acute sinus infections can make someone very sick and cause a headache, but people with frequent headaches in the sinus areas, who think that chronic sinus problems are the cause of their headaches, usually, in fact, have migraine. A recent study found that of over 2,500 patients who thought they had sinus headache, more than 90% had migraine headache. In addition, many people who worry that their headaches result from psychological factors seek treatment for sinus and allergy problems, which they would rather believe are the cause of their headaches.

The bulk of nonprescription pain medication is consumed by migraine sufferers and people with chronic daily headache. Headache sufferers are the main purchasers of the 20,000 tons of ASA (Aspirin), plus much of the acetaminophen (Tylenol), ibuprofen, and other anti-inflammatory and sinus medications, consumed yearly in the United States. Lacking a proper diagnosis, these individuals rely on off-the-shelf medicines because they have never received a prescription for a migraine-specific medication.

Until the middle of the twentieth century, *over the counter* meant that you could ask your pharmacist for a bottle of Aspirin, for example, and he or she would personally give it to you—over the counter. Today, only prescription medications are passed over the counter; nonprescription medicines are purchased *off the shelf* and are available in pharmacies, convenience stores, supermarkets, and gas stations (Figure 2-1).

Figure 2-1 Some off-the-shelf pain medications purchased without supervision.

As noted above, if nonprescription medication is used improperly, it can have serious consequences. *When overused*, ASA (Aspirin), specifically, and Excedrin Migraine and Anacin, both of which contain ASA, can cause or aggravate peptic ulcer, irritation of the stomach (gastritis), bleeding, bruising, ringing in the ears (tinnitus), and kidney damage; ASA can also aggravate asthma. Similarly, ibuprofen (Advil Migraine and Motrin Migraine Pain) can cause ulcers, bleeding, and kidney damage, and acetaminophen (Tylenol) can cause liver damage. Additionally, many sinus and allergy preparations contain ingredients that can increase your blood pressure.

At our Center in Stamford, CT, we frequently see patients who take 8 to 12 tablets per day of various off-the-shelf products. When the stronger prescription medications for headache are taken too frequently, the problem becomes worse. The more frequently a pain medication is taken, the greater is the risk of causing chronic severe headaches that respond poorly to all treatments. So, although off-the-shelf pain relievers and other medications targeted for headache can be effective when used properly for occasional headaches, overuse can result in headaches that are harder to treat, more painful, and more constant. These are called *analgesic rebound headaches*, *rebound headaches*, or *chronic migraine with medication overuse* (see Chapter 8).

The impact of headache on our society is enormous; migraine is truly a hidden epidemic. A Canadian survey shows that 92% of migraine sufferers have disability that ranges from diminished ability to function to requiring bed rest. Art created by headache sufferers has shown how headache can affect every aspect of their lives. Migraine victims feel isolated from the world around them at work, school, home, and play.

Headache is the leading cause of absenteeism from the workplace and accounts for the loss of some 150 million work days per year in the United States alone; the cost of lost labor hours is estimated to be as high as 17 billion dollars (US) each year. Headache can also disrupt every aspect of life outside the workplace and—in an era when some medical costs are not adequately covered by insurance companies—can result in unnecessary medical expense if misdiagnosed or inadequately treated.

Society may not understand headache or its impact on those who suffer from it. Workers who telephone their bosses or co-workers to say they cannot come to work because of a headache may be considered malingerers, or worse. The claim of disability because of the flu is more believable, and the claim of a broken bone is never questioned. Valerie South, of the International Headache Society, points out that "migraine is more than just a 'headache'; [it] is a debilitating disorder of the central nervous system."

Our mission is to educate you about headache so you can improve your quality of life and thereby decrease the impact of headache on you and your family. If you are one of the many migraine sufferers who have significant disability from migraine, this will be your first step toward decreasing the level of that disability and improving your functioning.

CHAPTER 3

TYPES OF HEADACHE

Headaches have been classified according to their characteristics to provide a common language for doctors and patients to use when talking about them.

All headaches can be classified as either primary or secondary. The secondary headache disorders are those caused by an underlying medical problem. Serious causes of secondary headache include brain tumors, bleeding in the brain, aneurysms (weakened blood vessel walls), and infections. Less serious causes of secondary headache include dental problems, temporomandibular joint (TMJ) syndrome, eye problems, true sinus infections, neck problems, and allergies. Although television commercials focus on allergies and sinus problems as causes of headache, the most common types of headaches are the primary headaches, whose causes are often not known. These are headaches not attributable to some other medical problem. The primary headache disorders fall into three main categories: (1) migraine, (2) tension-type headache, and (3) cluster headache (Table 3-1).

MIGRAINE

Migraine occurs three times more commonly in women than in men, often causing disability, and it affects about

Table 3-1 Major Headache Disorders	
Disorder	Prevalence (%)
Primary headache	
Migraine	12
Women	18
Men	6
Tension-type headache	70–90
Cluster	0.1
Secondary headache (organic)	<1

10 to 15% of the world's population. Most people with migraine have their first episode of headache between the ages of 6 and 25. Migraine occurs slightly more often in boys than in girls until the age of 11 or 12. After the onset of puberty, when girls start to menstruate, there is a higher incidence of migraine in girls and women. The two major categories of migraine are migraine without aura (previously called *common migraine* because it is the most common type) and migraine with aura (previously called *classic migraine,* which only about 30% of migraineurs ever experience). Migraine is usually inherited. Parents with migraine whose children complain of headache should not assume that their children are imitating them. Children of migraine sufferers who complain of headaches should be believed and evaluated by a doctor. Headache may begin as early as age 2. If one parent has migraine, there is about a 40% chance that each child will have it; if both parents have migraine, there is at least a 75% chance that each child will experience migraine.

Migraine without Aura

A simplified way of recognizing migraine is becoming popular with primary care phsyicians: any patient with a stable pattern over at least 6 months of intermittent severe headache in discrete episodes that causes disability or results in lost time from work, home, school, or recreational activities, with no worsening over time, has migraine until proven otherwise (Table 3-2).

Headache specialists also use specific criteria to make a diagnosis of migraine without aura: at least five previous

Table 3-2 Proposed Simplified Diagnosis of Migraine
A stable pattern of intermittent headache that causes at least some disability, with no worsening over time, is migraine until proven otherwise.

attacks should have occurred, underlying medical conditions or serious causes that could mimic migraine must be ruled out, and attacks must last for 4 to 72 hours, with an average attack lasting from 12 to 48 hours. With these criteria present, the diagnosis of migraine without aura then requires the presence of two of the four group A diagnostic characteristics and one of the three group B characteristics shown in Table 3-3.

Other symptoms of a migraine attack may include dizziness, frequent urination, diarrhea, sweating, and cold hands and feet. We describe some "red flags" in Chapter 5 that help you determine when to be concerned about other causes of headache. For example, if a fever is present with your headache, you must contact a doctor to rule out a serious infection such as meningitis. High blood pressure during a migraine attack may just be because of the pain, but it may be dangerous to take a triptan or other medications when your blood pressure is high. To be on the safe side, have your blood pressure checked between headaches to make sure it has returned to normal levels (for example, 110–120/70–80 mm Hg) and to be certain you do not have high blood pressure, which must be treated.

Many patients with an acute migraine attack retreat to a dark quiet room and lie very still; sleep may help to end a migraine attack.

Table 3-3 Diagnostic Characteristics of Migraine without Aura

Group A (two of four)
Headache on one side of the head
Throbbing or pulsating pain
Moderate to severe pain that makes it difficult or impossible to function
Worsening of pain in response to routine physical activity such as bending over or climbing stairs

Group B (one of three)
Nausea
Vomiting
Sensitivity to light and sound

Migraine with Aura

Aura refers to symptoms that are usually visual and occur before or at the same time as the headache. In fact the word *aura* means *wind*. Approximately 15 to 30% of patients with migraine experience the warning phenomenon of aura with some or all of their headaches. Headache that follows aura is similar to that previously described, but it is often less intense and not as difficult to treat.

Some patients have aura without the subsequent headache; this is known as a *migraine equivalent* or *aura without headache*. This does not have to be treated unless the auras are very frequent.

Auras usually last for 20 to 30 minutes. The most common types of visual auras are multicolored spots, flashing bright lights (photopsia), or bright-edged shimmering zigzag lines in the shape of a crescent (Figure 3-1). This shape can grow in size and move slowly across the visual field. Other visual disturbances include a scotoma (a small growing black or colorless area in the visual field) that obscures vision, loss of vision on one or both sides, tunnel vision, or inability to see words in a particular area when looking at a printed page. Some auras include neurologic events that can resemble stroke symptoms, such as weakness or numbness in

Figure 3-1 Visual aura — changes in vision prior to migraine pain.

an arm and/or leg on one side, difficulty speaking or thinking, coordination problems, or even loss of consciousness. If aura symptoms persist for more than 1 hour, they could be related to a more serious abnormality in the brain. Typically, the headache follows the aura either immediately or within 60 minutes.

TENSION-TYPE HEADACHE

Tension-type headache is the most common type of headache. Probably 90% or more of the world's population has experienced one from time to time. Many of these headaches are associated with tension in muscles in the head, face, jaw, or neck, although this may not be the case in some patients. There is much speculation as to whether tension-type headache and migraine headache are separate disorders. Many headache specialists believe they are caused by similar mechanisms in the brain, and most patients who experience one also experience the other. Tension-type headache may be episodic (occurring once in a while) or chronic (occuring most days of the month).

Episodic Tension-Type Headache

Occurring occasionally—once or twice per week or once per month—episodic tension-type headaches are described as a mild pressing, aching, squeezing sensation, or as a tight band around the head that does not throb or pound. They are usually felt on both sides of the head. Unlike migraine, the pain is often mild or moderate, does not interfere with normal function, and is not aggravated by activity. These headaches are not associated with nausea; however, light or sound sensitivity may be present, but not both.

Chronic Tension-Type Headache

Symptoms of chronic tension-type headache are identical to those of the episodic variety. However, chronic tension-type headache occurs on more than 15 days per month, usually almost daily. Many patients have had these symptoms for months or years when they first visit our office. They often eventually develop chronic daily headache, with pain on and off throughout each day.

Tension-type headache is really defined by what it is not—it is not migraine; it is a featureless headache. Tension-type headache, because it is not associated with impact on lifestyle or disability, does not bring a patient into the doctor's office. Notice that tension-type headache is not defined by a location in the neck or the side or back of the head. Headaches signficant enough to cause disability and lost time from life, but occurring in these locations, usually turn out to be migraine. So don't let the location of pain or its triggers alone determine your diagnosis!

CLUSTER HEADACHE

Cluster headache is probably the most dramatic of all the headache types. There are two categories of cluster headache: episodic cluster, which is more common (about 90% of cases), and chronic. Episodic cluster occurs for about 4 to 8 weeks and then disappears. In this cluster period, the patient experiences attacks about 1 to 3 times per day. Cluster periods may occur every 1 to 2 years or only once in a lifetime. Chronic cluster continues for years, and attacks occur at least several times per week.

The pain of cluster headache occurs exclusively on one side of the head, in and around the eye and temple. In contrast to typical throbbing migraine pain, cluster pain is more steady, boring, and relentless. Patients describe the pain as an intense pressure behind the eye that feels as though it is pushing the eye forward out of the socket. Some patients describe the feeling as one that makes them want to pluck out the painful eye. Others describe it as a red-hot poker being thrust into the eye with immense force and then twirled. Drooping of the eyelid, constriction of the pupil, and redness and tearing of the eye, followed by a stuffed then running nostril, may accompany the headache, all occurring on the same side of the head as the pain. Average duration of the pain is 45 to 90 minutes, but it may last anywhere from 20 minutes to 3 hours.

Attacks may occur several times per day, with an average of one to three attacks in a 24-hour period. Cluster headaches often occur at the same time of the day or night, almost like clockwork, usually after work. Most characteristically, these headaches awaken the sufferer 90 minutes after falling asleep. Patients notice that if they nap during the day they awaken with a headache.

In contrast to migraine, which affects one in five women and occurs three times more frequently in women than in men, cluster headache occurs five times as often in men and affects less than 0.1% of the population. A family history of cluster headache is much less common than it is with migraine. The typical sufferer is a 35-year-old male, a little taller than average, who may have hazel-colored eyes and deep lines around the forehead, mouth, and chin.

Cluster pain is so excruciating that it brings even the strongest of men to their knees. It is no wonder that cluster headache has been termed *suicide headache*. Rather than retreating to a dark quiet room, as do migraine sufferers, cluster patients cannot sit or lie still. Rather, they pace, rock, and drive their fists into the painful eye. Some patients may even show unusual behavior, such as hitting themselves in the head, banging their heads against the wall, or engaging in intense physical activity such as push-ups or running.

The word *cluster* describes the timing pattern of these headaches, which occur in cluster periods of about 4 to 8 weeks per year. Patients are free of headache between cluster periods. Alcohol is the most common trigger, but only during the cluster period. Frequent drinkers of alcohol may stop drinking completely until the cluster period has passed.

Symptoms and signs of cluster headache may mislead doctors to incorrect diagnoses, such as sinus headaches, and inappropriate treatments, such as a variety of sinus medications and surgery. They may also be mistaken for dental problems or TMJ dysfunction (see page 20). Many a patient with undiagnosed cluster headaches, whose pain centered around the upper rear molars, has had teeth extracted unnecessarily.

Fortunately, we now have effective treatments for cluster headaches to reduce the frequency and severity of the attacks (see Chapter 11). If the diagnosis is made, effective treatment usually follows.

OTHER TYPES OF HEADACHE

Exertional Headache
An exertional headache is brought on by physical effort of any type, including bending, coughing, sneezing, straining, exercise, and even sex. This type of headache should always be brought to a doctor's attention as underlying abnormalities of the brain, although not common, should be looked for carefully.

Ice Pick–Like Pains
Headache known officially as *idiopathic* (cause unknown) *stabbing headache* is perceived as very sharp, extremely brief ice pick–like pains or "jabs and jolts" at various locations in the head. They occur singly or in volleys over a few minutes and return at least occasionally or up to several times a day in about 40% of migraine patients. They can be always in the same place, but most often they move around. They are usually benign, and no cause is found.

Sex Headache

Sex headache or *coital headache* is an intense headache that occurs primarily in men at the time of orgasm, although it can occur in women, also. It is so severe that the first episode usually causes the patient to be taken to the emergency room. A series of tests should be performed to ensure that there is no underlying brain problem. If no cause is found, the headaches often stop occurring after several months. Indomethacin, a nonsteroidal anti-inflammatory medication, taken either before having sex or on a daily basis, is frequently helpful in decreasing or stopping the pain (see above).

Episodic and Chronic Paroxysmal Hemicrania

Episodic and chronic paroxysmal hemicrania is a rare type of headache disorder that resembles cluster headache. Unlike cluster headache, it occurs more commonly in women than in men and is characterized by more than five brief attacks per day. The pain, which is always one sided in and around an eye, lasts for only 5 to 10 minutes, is excruciatingly severe, and is associated with at least one of the following autonomic signs: a red eye, tearing eye, drooping eyelid, small pupil, or stuffed or running nostril, all on the same side as the pain.

Migraine variants occur frequently in some patients. Exertional headaches, ice pick–like pains, and the paroxysmal hemicranias may respond to the nonsteroidal anti-inflammatory medication indomethacin (Indocin), 25 to 50 mg three times per day. Indomethacin is available by prescription.

"Ice Cream Headache"

The official term for ice cream headache is *cold stimulus headache* because it occurs after you eat or drink something very cold such as ice cream. It lasts for fewer than 5 minutes, is located between the eyes, and may be prevented by eating ice

Figure 3-2 A young boy about to experience an "ice-cream headache."

cream slowly and in small amounts and by letting it melt in the mouth before swallowing (Figure 3-2). It may be more prevalent in migraineurs.

Chronic Daily Headache

At present, there is no official classification for *daily* (frequently constant) *headache*, but we often use this term. Studies show a prevalence of 4 to 5% of chronic daily headache in the US population. Often, patients say that it waxes and wanes throughout the day, but that even when it is not bothering them, it is present. It wears them down. Occasionally, the pain becomes sufficiently severe that it interferes with their ability to function. This type of headache clearly resembles migraine on some days, sometimes frequently. Some experts believe these patients have transformed or chronic migraine, which starts in the teens with occasional migraine attacks and transforms to daily waxing and waning pain (mild, moderate, or severe) by the time they are in their thirties and forties. Eighty percent of people with chronic daily headache seen in most doctors' offices take pain relievers or other acute care medications (such as triptans) on a daily basis. This can result in rebound headache or chronic migraine with medication overuse. The current thinking is that the overuse of these medications prevents the brain's natural pain-fighting mechanisms from working. The result is more frequent and severe headaches that do not respond to the usually effective medications (see Chapter 8). Intense carefully designed treatment can be helpful.

Post-traumatic Headache

Post-traumatic headaches are caused by injury to the head or neck and may even develop after what seems to be only a minor injury. These headaches usually occur on both sides of the head; they are constant, mild to moderate in intensity, and can continue for months. The great majority of people who suffer a head or neck injury in an automobile accident or strike their heads on a low beam have a headache for 48 hours to a few weeks. Sometimes the headaches become severe or even incapacitating, lasting for months or years and resemble migraine. Patients with post-traumatic headache may be thought to be exaggerating their pain or malingering, but in our experience, these patients have a debilitating disorder that may destroy the fabric of their lives and seriously impair their ability to function for years.

Some patients with post-traumatic headache also develop post–head trauma syndrome and experience impaired concentration, memory, and sleep, as well as irritability, decreased energy and interests, inability to perform sexually, personality changes, and decreased ability to handle even simple tasks.

Although diagnostic tests such as scans of the brain or the cervical spine and electroencephalograms fail to reveal abnormalities, the injury may have caused microscopic tearing and damage to nerve fibers in the brain, brainstem, and spine, as well as metabolic changes. The damage may disrupt the delicate balance of the chemical messengers that control pain. Many patients develop post-traumatic headache as a result of whiplash (a neck injury) after a car accident in which they were rear-ended. The degree of head trauma does not necessarily correlate with the degree of pain intensity or disability. Preexisting migraine or tension-type headache may worsen after this kind of injury.

"Sinus Headache"

Sinus problems rarely cause chronic headaches. The term *sinus headache* was invented by advertisers to sell decongestants and over-the-counter antihistamines. In fact Ear, Nose, and Throat doctors do not recognize *sinus headaches* in their list of diagnoses. Rather, they note that headache can sometimes occur as a minor symptom accompanying infections of the sinuses, that is, acute sinusitis. Blockage of the sinus drainage system may cause infection, and these infections are classified as acute or chronic sinusitis. Headache caused by acute sinusitis may be felt in the cheeks or below, above, or behind the eyes, or may be referred to other areas such as the teeth or the top of the head (Figure 3-3).

Acute sinusitis is generally associated with fever, red-hot

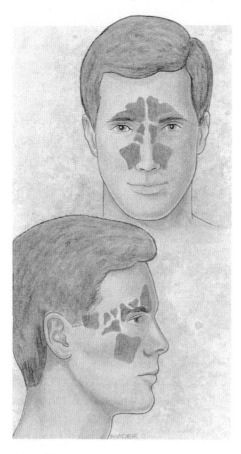

Figure 3-3 Diagram of sinuses in the head and face.

skin over the sinus, and a yellow-green bad-tasting or -smelling discharge from the nostrils and back of the throat. Any headache associated with fever or infection must be treated immediately.

Chronic low-grade inflammation of any of the sinuses in the head may rarely cause headache. The pain patterns are similar to those in acute sinusitis but of lesser intensity and not usually associated with fever. Depending on the sinuses involved, pain may be increased by shaking the head or by lying in certain positions that decrease the ability of the sinuses to drain. A severe sinus problem may trigger a migraine attack. However, most patients who think they have chronic sinus headache do not.

Dr. Roger Cady, a headache specialist and family practitioner in Springfield, MO, recently did a study in which he advertised in the newspaper for people with self-diagnosed sinus headache. Ninety-six percent of people who responded actually had migraine or probable migraine. Thus, disabling headaches that last for 1 to 3 days, occur several times per month, and are associated with weather triggers, nasal stuffiness, clear drainage, tearing eyes, or postnasal drip are usually migraine.

Allergy Headache
Commercials and advertisements to the contrary, most headaches are not brought on by allergies. Rarely, allergy to pollen and grasses and hay fever can cause sinus pain and headache if the sinuses fill up because of the allergic reaction.

Eye-Related Headache
Eye strain is not a common cause of chronic or recurrent headache. Headaches that are due to eye strain are generally mild and are felt in the forehead or in the eyes themselves. The pain is absent on awakening and worsens when the eyes are used for prolonged periods. Children with headaches are

usually checked early on for eye problems, which often are not found.

Glaucoma (increased pressure within the eye) may cause a headache that mimics a bad migraine or tension-type headache, or it may cause severe pain in and around the eye or in the forehead. If you notice changes in your vision, especially if you see halos around lights, accompanied by pain and other symptoms, consult an eye doctor at once.

Headache Caused by TMJ Dysfunction

The TMJ is located just in front of the ear, where the jaw meets the skull. TMJ problems may cause ear or jaw pain, ringing in the ears, clicking in the joint, or pain (headache) in the area where the hinges of the jaw meet the upper face. Many patients have been misdiagnosed as having TMJ problems and have undergone major surgical reconstruction of the joint without experiencing any relief of their pain. Most "TMJ headaches" are actually migraine or tension-type headaches. Some patients grind their teeth at night, and that can be a cause of early-morning headache.

Trigeminal Neuralgia

Trigeminal neuralgia is a piercing sudden-onset severe pain that lasts for 1 to 4 minutes and is confined to the cheek, jaw, or rarely the forehead on one side of the face. This type of pain is triggered by talking, chewing, exposure to wind, or even by touching the face. It can continue daily for many months and then often disappears for a while. It comes from a problem with the trigeminal nerve and is treated with medication and, on rare occasions, surgery.

Spinal Tap Headache

Spinal tap headache occurs 12 to 48 hours after a diagnostic spinal tap (lumbar puncture), in which fluid is removed from the spinal column. It is a diffuse steady pain in the head and neck accompanied by nausea. It gets worse upon standing and disappears upon lying down. The headache occurs because fluid leaks from the spinal column at the spot where the needle puncture was made. The treatment is to drink sufficient fluids and to lie absolutely flat for 2 days. This type of headache disappears slowly. In severe cases a minor procedure called an epidural blood patch is performed to seal the hole and prevent further leakage of spinal fluid.

CONCLUSION

There are other types of headache, some probably not yet discovered, but after reading this chapter you should have a good idea what type of headaches you have. Many people have more than one type.

CHAPTER 4

CAUSES OF HEADACHE

Our patients frequently ask us, "What causes my headaches?" Another frequently asked question is, "If all my tests are normal, and nothing's seriously wrong, why do I get headaches?"

Understandably, patients with unexplained symptoms fear the worst, and when most causes of headache have been ruled out, they may fall back on media-driven explanations that attribute headache to sinus, allergy, and stress-related problems. It is not surprising that when test results are normal many patients fear their headaches are not real but, rather, the result of a psychological process. This is not usually the case.

Unfortunately, there are no biologic markers or accurate tests to confirm the diagnosis of the most common headache disorders. Diagnosis of headache is based on a detailed medical history, neurologic and physical examinations, and appropriate tests. Most causes of headache probably do not show up on routine tests because we do not yet have the specific means to measure biochemical and electrical changes in the brain, the blood vessels, and the muscles. Special testing is not always necessary; sometimes headache is diagnosable by history and examination.

CAUSES OF MIGRAINE

The tendency to develop migraine is inherited; up to 90% of people with migraine have a close relative who gets them, too. Your family history can give your doctor important information that may suggest migraine as a diagnosis. Some studies show that if one parent has migraine, each child has a 40% chance of developing it; if both parents have migraine, each child has a 75% chance.

Four main theories about the cause of migraine have been proposed. The theories center on the following: (1) the brain (the central theory); (2) the blood vessels (the vascular theory); (3) inflammation (the neurogenic inflammation theory, which involves the trigeminovascular system) (Figure 4-1); and (4) a combination of these factors (the unifying theory), which pulls the three interrelated theories together.

The Brain: Central Theory

Different experts in headache have different theories on the cause of migraine; these ideas are not mutually exclusive. One widely accepted belief is that the migraine brain is too easily excited. According to this theory of a "sensitive" or "hyperexcitable" brain, nerve cells in the brain fire too easily and thereby start the migraine attack. A variety of internal and external trigger factors cause the brain to wind up into a migraine; some triggers are readily apparent (such as fatigue, lack of sleep, too much sleep, stress, the weather, and menses), whereas other factors are never found. But the critical understanding is that it is not the triggers that cause the migraine but rather the irritable nerve cells in the brain.

Dr. K.M.A. Welch, from the University of Kansas, Kansas City, KS, and Dr. Nabih Ramadan, a neurologist and clinical research scientist in Indianapolis, IN, observed that magnesium levels in the brain are low in migraine patients. One theory holds that low magnesium levels may be a cause of abnormal brain electrical activity that starts in the back of the brain during the visual aura phase and spreads forward. This happens because low magnesium levels allow microscopic channels in the membranes that cover a nerve cell to open and let calcium come into the cell. This increases the irritability of the cell producing the electrical change.

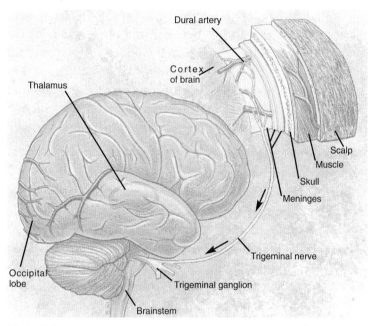

Figure 4-1 Anatomy of brain and scalp showing the trigeminovascular system.

Another area of the brain that may be hyperexcitable is the lowest part, called the *brainstem* (see Figure 4-1). Nerve cells in the brainstem contain a large amount of a chemical called *serotonin* that regulates pain. Dr. Neil Raskin, a professor of neurology at the University of California in San Francisco, CA, believes that headache results from a disturbance of serotonin activity in the midbrain, which is the upper part of the brainstem. The fact that several medications effective in migraine affect serotonin receptors suggests that this may be the case.

The Blood Vessels: Vascular Theory

In the seventeenth century, Sir Thomas Willis proposed that migraine was caused by changes in blood vessel activity, a theory updated at The New York Hospital during the 1930s by Drs. Harold Wolff and John Graham. The fact that ergotamine tartrate given intravenously noticeably decreased the painful throbbing and pulsations of swollen arteries in the scalp supported this theory. However, ergotamine and its descendents, the newer triptans, also work on serotonin receptors to turn off migraine, but this was not known at the time. It is not clear whether the blood vessel–constricting effects are necessary for antimigraine drug action, or whether the nerve effects are sufficient.

The Trigeminovascular System: Neurogenic Inflammation Theory

Dr. Michael Moskowitz, a professor of neurology at Harvard Medical School in Boston, MA, has shown that the trigeminovascular system of the brain is the key pathway of migraine pain. This system involves 1 of the 12 cranial nerves—the trigeminal (or fifth cranial nerve)—and its connections between the arteries in the covering of the brain (the meninges) and the nerve cells in the brainstem. Chemicals released from the peripheral ends of the trigeminal nerve cause inflammation to occur around blood vessels. Many medicines effective in treating migraine—including the triptans and ergotamine (see Chapter 9)—act at the interface of the trigeminal nerve endings and the vascular system in the meninges by reducing the release of these irritating chemicals and thereby decreasing the pain.

Unifying Theory

Dr. James Lance, a professor of neurology and well-known headache specialist in Sydney, Australia, believes that migraine represents a succession of events that begins in one area in the back of the brain as an electrical change and causes alterations in another area of the brain and the trigeminovascular system. These changes trigger biochemical events in the brain that result in clumping of platelets, alterations in blood vessel size, and release of pain-producing substances.

One way to understand this unification of ideas is to think of migraine as a process occurring in a "central generator" in the upper brainstem that is set wrongly so that it fires too easily. When this switch turns on, nerves fire and activate the trigeminovascular system causing inflammation and blood vessel dilation to occur in the meninges. From there the pain signal goes back into the brainstem where it is integrated and where nausea and other migraine symptoms are generated. Therefore, migraine occurs as a three-step process:

1. Activation of the migraine central generator in the brainstem
2. Activation of the peripheral pain mechanism, which is caused by inflammation, and blood vessel dilation in the meninges
3. Reentry of the pain signal into the brain for integration and initiation of nausea and other migraine symptoms, which last until the central generator switch turns off

Recent research at the Beth Israel Hospital and Harvard Medical School in Boston by Dr. Rami Burstein from Israel shows the windup in the brainstem (called *central sensitization*) and suggests that the sooner a migraine attack is stopped by medication, the less severe that attack will be.

As you can see, much progress has been made that is beginning to shed more light on our understanding of migraine as a neurologic disorder.

MIGRAINE TRIGGERS

As noted above, triggers are not the cause of migraine but, rather, turn on the central switch. Many migraine patients are unusually sensitive to internal (within the body) and external (outside the body) environmental changes (Table 4-1). A variety of factors can trigger an explosive migraine attack (Figure 4-2). The menstrual cycle is clearly a major

Table 4-1 Triggers of Migraine
Internal
Chronic fatigue, too little sleep
Emotional stress, let-down after stress
Hormonal fluctuations (menstrual cycle)
External
Weather and seasonal change
Travel through time zones (see Chapter 17)
Altitude
Skipping or delaying meals
Sensory stimuli
Flickering or bright lights, sunlight
Odors, including perfume, chemicals, cigarette smoke
Heat, loud noises
Medications (see Chapter 9)
Nitroglycerin
Tetracycline (an antibiotic)
High doses of vitamin A
Some antidepressant medications (selective serotonin reuptake inhibitors)
Some blood pressure medications

trigger in the great majority of women; a second trigger is food. Although alcoholic beverages are common triggers, red wine, beer, and champagne are the drinks most frequently mentioned by patients. The dark-colored alcohols (scotch, bourbon, dark rum, and red wine) appear more likely to trigger migraine attacks than the light-colored ones (gin, vodka, white rum, and white wine). Many foods (Table 4-2), particularly those that contain tyramine, trigger migraine, but only in some people.

Monosodium glutamate (MSG), an ingredient added to a wide variety of preserved and frozen foods, can trigger migraine. Read food labels carefully. Look not only for *MSG* but for the words *hydrolyzed fat* or *hydrolyzed protein*. Both Nutrasweet, a food ingredient, and Equal, a sugar substitute, contain aspartame, and both have been associated with headache in susceptible individuals, especially if they are taken in large amounts (several diet sodas or other aspartame-containing foods per day).

Caffeine is a double-edged sword. Since caffeine may help constrict the dilated blood vessels during a migraine attack, it is used in combination medicines to increase relief from headache (for example, Excedrin Migraine is a combination of ASA, acetaminophen, and caffeine; Fiorinal contains caffeine; Cafergot contains caffeine). However, habitual consumption of too much caffeine can make headaches worse. How much caffeine is too much? Some patients are sensitive to the small amount of caffeine (approximately 100 mg) in one small (5 oz) cup of brewed coffee.

Figure 4-2 Triggers that set off the explosion of migraine.

Many patients who complain of headaches on

Table 4-2 Dietary Triggers		
Chocolate	Onions	Nutrasweet, Equal (aspartame)
Nuts	Pizza	Canned figs
Peanut butter	Avocado	Aged cheese
Bananas	Processed meats	Caffeine (see Table 4-3)
Alcoholic beverages	Hot dogs, pepperoni,	
Red wine	sausages, bacon, ham,	
Others	bologna, salami	
	Pickled/fermented foods	
	Yogurt	
	Sour cream	

Saturday or Sunday mornings intake less caffeine on weekends than during the week, or they sleep later and therefore drink their coffee later in the morning. Headaches that occur under these circumstances could be due to caffeine withdrawal and are more likely to occur in people who are accustomed to drinking more than 300 mg of caffeine per day (about three cups of coffee). At 500 mg per day or above, caffeinism, with symptoms that include disturbed sleep, anxiety, nervousness, rapid or irregular heartbeat, and irritability, may occur. Table 4-3 lists the caffeine content of various products and foods.

Table 4-3 Caffeine Content of Common Foods and Drugs		
Product	Example	Caffeine Content (mg)
Cocoa and chocolate	Chocolate candy bar	25
	Cocoa beverage (175 mL mixture)	10
Coffee	Decaffeinated (150 mL)	2
	Drip (150 mL)	146
	Instant, regular (150 mL)	53
	Percolated (150 mL)	110
Tea	3-minute brew (150 mL)	22–46
Off-the-shelf drugs	Anacin	32
	Extra-Strength Excedrin	65
	Excedrin Migraine	65
	No-Doz tablets	100–200
	Vanquish	33
	Vivarin tablets	200
Prescription drugs	Darvon Compound-65	32
	Esgic	40
	Fioricet	40
	Fiorinal	40
Soft drinks (350 mL)	7-Up/Diet 7-Up	0
	Coca-Cola	34
	Diet Coke	45
	Dr. Pepper	41

Stress

Although stress is high on the list of migraine triggers, stress does not usually cause migraine headaches in those who are not biologically predisposed to migraine. When stress does cause a headache, it is usually a tension-type headache and should decrease as soon as the stress lessens. Migraine is likely to occur during letdown periods, such as after the stress has come and gone, or during a period of unwinding or relaxing. This may explain why many patients have migraine attacks on weekends or on vacations.

CAUSES OF TENSION-TYPE HEADACHE

Early theories of causes of tension-type headache attributed the pain to contraction of muscles around the head and neck, which explains why this type of headache was originally termed *muscle contraction headache*. It is true that tension-type headache may occur in people who—for one reason or another—unconsciously tighten up the muscles around the head, neck, and shoulders. All of the following may also be triggers of tension-type headache: poor posture, tense jaw, temporomandibular joint problems, arthritis, disc disease in the neck, and occupational factors, such as sitting for long periods at computer terminals, typing, or cradling the phone between the ear and shoulder.

It is easy to understand how tight muscles could be related to tension-type headache, but factors within the brain may be involved as well; tension-type headache may have nothing to do with muscles or tension in some patients.

POSSIBLE CONNECTIONS BETWEEN TENSION-TYPE HEADACHE AND MIGRAINE

Since some of the symptoms of tension-type headache and migraine overlap, and since many people suffer from both types of headache, several headache specialists believe that these two conditions are related. Many patients may develop an acute tension-type headache that, over a period of hours, evolves into a clear-cut migraine. It is not surprising that one group of headache specialists believes that headaches represent a continuum that includes tension-type headache and migraine, which share similar underlying mechanisms. Another group considers the two headache types to be completely distinct disorders. A third and newer theory is that tension-type headache that occurs in migraine sufferers is really just low-level migraine, whereas tension-type headache in people who do not get migraine is a distinct and separate type of headache. Dr. Roger Cady, a family practitioner and director of the Primary Care Network in Springfield, MO, and Dr. Richard Lipton, a professor of neurology and public health at the Albert Einstein College of Medicine in New York, NY, have provided recent evidence that supports this third hypothesis.

Depression and anxiety are often associated with chronic daily headache, tension-type headache, and migraine and should be addressed as part of a patient's entire headache picture. Some patients with depression and anxiety need behavioral treatment from a psychologist, and some may need medication.

CAUSES OF CLUSTER HEADACHE

The causes of cluster headache are complex. According to Dr. Lee Kudrow, a well-known retired internist and headache specialist in Beverly Hills, CA, a tiny nerve bundle that regulates body rhythms deep within the hypothalamus of the brain is responsible for bringing on cluster headaches with clocklike regularity each day. It may also bring them back the same week the following year. Further evidence for involvement of this deep area of the brain was provided by Dr. Peter Goadsby, a professor of neurology at the National

Hospital at Queen Square, London, England, and his colleagues by means of specialized brain scanning (positron emission tomography [PET] scanning) when they found the "central generator" for cluster headache to be in the hypothalamus. Lithium carbonate has provided effective treatment for some patients, perhaps because it is believed to regulate the hypothalamus, which houses the body's biologic clock. Cluster headache also involves certain blood vessels and causes a hyperactivity of the parasympathetic nerves, which results in the red and tearing eye and the stuffed or running nostril that are associated with the pain.

Exciting new experimental treatment of cluster headache has been investigated by two neurologist-headache specialists in Milan, Italy, Drs. Gennaro Bussone and Massimo Leone suggested that electrodes be placed in the brain deep into the hypothalamus in their 6 toughest cluster headache patients who did not respond to any therapy. They all had a cessation of pain some time after the electrical simulation began. Further research may show this technique to be useful in our most difficult to treat cluster headache patients.

CONCLUSION

Further clarification of the biologic mechanisms responsible for headache will help doctors to understand more about headache and will yield more specific treatments that clinicians can offer to their patients. The next decade should bring answers as to how migraine is inherited and hopefully how to prevent it from starting.

CHAPTER 5

DANGER SIGNALS

More than 95% of headaches are primary headaches that are not caused by serious underlying medical conditions. You should, however, be aware of the "red flags" or danger signals listed below because these are signs that you should seek medical attention.

Consult a doctor if you experience any of the following:

- You rarely get headaches and suddenly develop a severe one
- You often get headaches and develop a new type or one that comes on suddenly and remains severe
- You develop the worst headache you have ever had
- You are over 40 years old and start to develop headache for the first time
- You develop a headache that gradually worsens over a period of days or weeks
- You get headaches when you exercise, cough, sneeze, strain having a bowel movement or during other strenuous activities, have sex, or bend over (They could be exertional migraine or benign exertional headaches, but you may have something more serious.)
- You get a "bug" or virus, and you develop a severe headache accompanied by nausea and vomiting and a neck so stiff that you cannot put your chin on your chest without pain. You must seek medical attention right away to rule out meningitis or hemorrhage.
- You get a headache accompanied by any of the following neurologic symptoms: trouble with coordination, double vision, weakness or numbness in any extremity or on one side of the body, drowsiness, inability to stay awake, confusion, impaired speech, or a change in personality

In general a new-onset headache in someone who does not usually get headaches, a headache much more severe than usual, a significant change in a typical headache, or a headache that escalates in severity more rapidly than usual or steadily over many days should be evaluated medically as soon as possible.

CHAPTER 6

THE DOCTOR'S ROLE

When you visit your own physician or a neurologist or headache specialist, you should be questioned carefully about your headaches. The doctor should ask about each type of headache you have and request details, such as the following: When did it start? How frequently do you get this type of headache? How long does it last? How does it impact on your life? Where is the pain located? How severe is it? Are there other symptoms associated with it such as nausea, vomiting, and sensitivity to light and sound? What brings it on (triggers it)? What makes it better? What is your behavior like during the headache?

Your doctor will then do a physical and neurologic examination and evaluate your mental alertness; cranial nerve function, including vision and hearing, and strength and sensation of the face; strength, coordination, and walking; reflexes; and ability to perceive different sensations. In addition, your blood pressure, pulse, neck motion, and the state of the arteries in your head and neck will be evaluated (Figure 6-1).

Although the histories of migraine sufferers are dramatic, most people usually turn out to have basically normal neurologic examinations. In fact people with migraine and tension-type headache *should* have normal examinations; if the examination is abnormal, the doctor will become concerned that another process may be causing the headaches.

Even if your examination is normal, your doctor may order blood tests to check for infection and inflammation, metabolic problems, liver or thyroid dysfunction, and perhaps for Lyme disease, anemia, and other conditions that might contribute to your headaches. Do not be surprised if your doctor sends you for a computed tomography (CT) scan, a magnetic resonance imaging (MRI) scan of your head, or even a magnetic resonance angiography (MRA) since these are the best ways to rule out serious structural problems in the brain. CT, MRI, and MRA scans are painless. CT scans involve the use of x-rays; an iodine-containing dye may be injected into an arm vein to increase the contrast of the images. Be sure to tell your doctor if you are allergic to iodine. MRI scans and MRAs do not use x-rays; rather they are done in a strong magnetic field. Another type of dye may be injected into an arm vein. Most MRI machines resemble a small tunnel, open at both ends (Figure 6-2). MRI scans usually cost more than do CT scans, but they provide more detailed information about more areas of the brain. Pregnant women should not undergo either scan, but an MRI scan is preferable to a CT scan

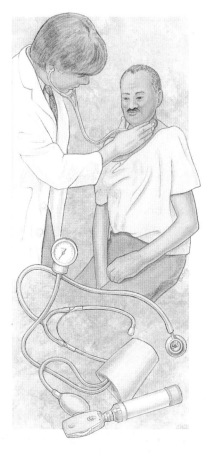

Figure 6-1 The neurologic examination should include listening for abnormal sounds (bruits) in the neck.

when imaging is necessary. For patients who are claustrophobic, open MRI scanners are less threatening. Health maintenance organizations (HMOs) and managed care companies sometimes try not to cover some of these expensive tests, but if they are essential, your doctor should be able to convince the company of their importance.

A spinal tap (lumbar puncture) may be indicated if your headaches are severe and are associated with a stiff neck, fever,

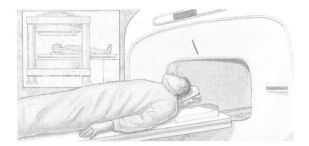

Figure 6-2 Magnetic resonance imaging (MRI) scanner.

vomiting, and signs of increased pressure in the brain. The most important abnormal findings from a spinal tap are evidence of bleeding, infection, or increased pressure. Patients are often told to lie flat for several hours after a spinal tap to avoid an increase in headache pain. An electroencephalography, during which many wires are attached to the scalp, can be useful when evaluating headache patients whose histories include fainting, loss of consciousness, seizures, head trauma, or dizziness.

The most important part of your evaluation is the history your doctor obtains from you. It alone can point to an accurate tentative diagnosis that can be confirmed by appropriate examination and testing. So prepare your history in advance by writing down all your symptoms, the tests you have had, and the medications you have tried. Bring in calendars you have kept and lists of medications and reports of tests.

Be sure to tell your doctor the impact your headaches have on your life. If there are times that, due to your headaches, you are unable to work, go to school, do household chores, or participate in family and social activities—or can only do these activities at a decreased level of efficacy—discuss these issues with your doctor early in your visit.

Most of the time, if the history and examination are complete and detailed at the first visit, a treatment plan can be begun immediately.

CHAPTER 7

PSYCHOLOGICAL FACTORS

Until recently the biologic basis of head pain was poorly understood and many headache sufferers were thought to have psychological problems as the basis of their headaches. Some still view psychiatric disorders as the primary causes of chronic pain and headache. This may be why headache is still not always considered a legitimate complaint and why some patients with headache are not taken seriously. We do not have all the answers, but we do know that headache has a firm basis in the neurobiology of the brain.

Although psychological factors, such as personality style, depression, anxiety, and stress, can influence headache, they rarely are the cause of it. All medical disorders, however, are affected by psychological factors. We cannot completely separate our minds from our bodies.

Psychological factors fall into three categories: (1) those that *do* cause headache (they are the least common cause), (2) those that contribute to it, and (3) those that coexist with it.

FACTORS THAT CAUSE HEADACHE

Psychogenic Factors

The term *psychogenic* suggests that the pain is either not real or that it is somehow different from real pain. The patient is not making it up, but there is no obvious physical cause of the pain.

Malingering

Malingering is the intentional production of false symptoms, in other words, conscious lying or faking. It may occur in drug or substance abusers or when people trying to avoid situations they do not like, such as school, work, jail, or combat duty. However, malingerers are rare, despite the misconception that people often fake head pain after experiencing trauma. Patients who have headache after car accidents usually have physiological causes of the headache, not psychological ones.

Migraine Personality

The term *migraine personality* has generated much confusion. The origin of the term is attributed to Dr. Harold Wolff, a neurologist working at The New York Hospital, NY, in the early 1960s, who noticed that a large percentage of his migraine patients seemed to have strikingly similar personality characteristics. However, according to Dr. Randall Weeks, a director of The New England Insitute of Behavioral Medicine in Stamford, CT, we know that the personalities of migraine sufferers differ very little from those of the rest of the population. There are people without headache that appear to have the migraine personality, and there are those with migraine that do not have it.

FACTORS THAT CONTRIBUTE TO HEADACHE

We believe that the common primary headache disorders are neurobiologic in origin and are genetically determined. Once a patient has the biologic vulnerability to develop headache, behavioral changes and stress may trigger one or make one worse.

Stress

The body is subject to stress when called upon to react to changes in the environment. When stress is overwhelming or constant, physical or emotional symptoms may occur. Areas of stress include difficulties at the workplace, marital problems, illness, financial problems, difficulty in school, and caring for a sick relative. Stress is not always negative, however. Positive events such as purchasing a house, getting married, having a child, moving, or changing jobs can be stressful, too.

Migraine patients often do well when they are going at "full speed." They may, however, develop migraine after the stress is resolved and they begin to relax; this explains why some patients experience attacks on weekends, during vacations, and when projects are completed. Patients suffering from cluster headaches tend to get their headaches after a nap or during the letdown time after work, when they are relaxing after a hard day. This is not a psychological phenomenon but one that can be explained by changes in brain chemistry.

PSYCHIATRIC DISORDERS THAT COEXIST WITH HEADACHE

Migraine and related disorders do not protect an individual from developing psychiatric problems or other physical problems. The prevalence of depression, anxiety disorders such as panic attacks, phobias, and sleep disorders is higher in patients with migraine and chronic daily headache. Although the exact relationship between head pain, anxiety, sleep disorders, and depression is not completely understood, we do know that serotonin, a chemical that occurs naturally in the brain, plays a role. The "serotonin connection" suggests that all these disorders share an underlying biologic cause.

There is some evidence that migraine, depression, and anxiety are sometimes inherited together. Studies by Professor Naomi Breslau at the Henry Ford Hospital in Detroit, MI, show that migraineurs experience more depression and that depressed patients have more migraines. Table 7-1 lists some common symptoms of depression and anxiety disorders. If you experience symptoms of anxiety or depression, you may want to consider the possibility that you have a treatable psychological problem.

Head pain is the depressed patient's most frequent physical complaint. Patients with chronic daily headache may also have depressive symptoms that include difficulty sleeping,

Table 7-1 Common Symptoms of Depression and Anxiety

Depression
  Depressed mood
  Decreased ability to experience pleasure, and decreased interests
  Significant changes in weight
  Persistent difficulty in falling asleep or staying asleep
  Sleeping too much
  Others have observed that you are markedly slowed
    down or agitated
  Decreased energy or increased fatigue
  Feelings of worthlessness, guilt, decreased concentration, and inability to
    make even simple decisions
  Recurrent thoughts of death
Anxiety
  Shortness of breath or a feeling of smothering
  Dizziness or feelings of unsteadiness
  Palpitations or rapid heart beat
  Trembling or shaking
  Sweating
  Choking or trouble swallowing
  Nausea or abdominal distress
  A feeling that you are not real or that your environment is somehow not
    real or changed
  Numbness or tingling sensations
  Chills or flushing
  Chest pain
  Fear of dying
  Fear of going crazy or doing something that you cannot control

decreased interest in everything they formerly enjoyed, decreased energy, and decreased concentration. If depression or anxiety coexist with your headache disorder, it is difficult to treat one without addressing the other. Do not be upset if your doctor suggests that you may be anxious or depressed. He or she is trying to manage all the factors that may contribute to your headache. You may be surprised to learn that headache specialists frequently prescribe antidepressant medications, even if the patient is not depressed. These medications raise your serotonin levels and can work against headache, depression, anxiety, and sleep problems.

CONCLUSION

Psychological factors may contribute to your headaches, but they are rarely the cause. A variety of psychological tests may help to identify depression and anxiety. Other disorders such as alcoholism and other forms of drug or substance abuse must be identified as well. Although many headache patients may overuse medication, they are not often substance abusers; rather, they use medications in an effort to remain functional and to decrease their pain. The end result is not usually good, however. Overuse of pain medication, caffeine, and other acute care headache medications, such as ergots and triptans, can lead to analgesic rebound headache, a condition in which the overused medications result in daily or near-daily headache. More information about analgesic rebound headache is presented in Chapter 8.

REBOUND HEADACHE

Headaches can be made more severe, more constant, and more difficult to treat by overuse of off-the-shelf and pre-scription pain relievers such as ASA and acetaminophen, bar-biturates, opiates, caffeine, ergotamine tartrate, and even the triptans. Overuse often results in analgesic rebound headache. In addition some medications prescribed for med-ical conditions other than headache may worsen or produce headache. If you have headache and take a lot of medication, ask your doctor if any of them could be contributing to your headache problem.

ANALGESIC REBOUND HEADACHE

Increasing your consumption of pain medication not only usually fails to relieve headache, it may perpetuate and inten-sify it. This is known as *analgesic rebound headache* or *chronic migraine with medication overuse* or *transformed migraine* because the headaches "transform" from discrete episodes into a daily or near-daily pattern. Most headache specialists agree that taking prescription pain medications more than 3 days in a week greatly increases the risk of developing rebound headache. What's more, taking off-the-shelf medications— even as few as two to four tablets every day just 3 to 4 days a week—can also produce the problem. Many patients who develop rebound headache take more than one kind of pain reliever. Headache medicines are often a combination of products (see Chapter 9) that include a variety of pain reliev-ers, caffeine, and other substances that affect blood vessels. Almost every medication taken acutely for headache used more than 3 days per week can cause rebound. Even ASA and acetaminophen and maybe the nonsteroidal anti-inflammatory medications—alone or in combination, with or without caffeine—cause rebound. Two of the more common ingredients, in addition to caffeine, that are included in as-needed medications and that cause rebound headache are butalbital, which is in Fiorinal, Fioricet, Phrenilin, and Esgic; and codeine, which is in Fiorinal with codeine, Fioricet with codeine, Tylenol with codeine, and similar preparations sold under various brand and generic names. Other sedatives and tranquilizers may also cause rebound headache. Additionally, overuse of these medications tends to reduce the usual effectiveness of daily preventive medications, "designer" migraine-specific acute care medications such as triptans, relaxation techniques, and biofeedback training. Daily caffeine intake from beverages and mixed analgesics may also contribute to the headache problem (see page 46).

So how does overuse of pain medications come about? Let's say you often wake up in the morning with a mild headache that you are afraid will get worse. To be on the "safe side," you take a small dose of an off-the-shelf pain reliever every morning. Before long you are taking two pills every 4 hours—or 6 to 12 tablets a day. Over time your headaches seem to get worse; this leads you to increase the number of pills you take. Before you know it, you are taking large amounts of medication and, instead of feeling better, you feel much worse.

Rebound can also result from use of an ineffective prescription medication for disabling migraine. If you have disabling migraine, it is better to treat your attacks with migraine-specific medication such as triptans right from the start of your therapy. If your physician gives you a low-level nonspecific medication and instructs you to take it when you get a migraine, the low-level medication is unlikely to make you pain free or even better. If you are not pain free with the nonspecific medication, your migraine is likely to recur; this leads to re-treatment with the low-level medication. Soon a cycle of treatment, medication wear off, withdrawal, headache, and re-treatment sets in. This is the basis of rebound. Rebound headaches often occur in the early morning as the medication has worn off through the night.

Patients may become anxious and depressed, may have difficulty falling asleep, or even more commonly may awaken between 2:00 and 4:00 am and be unable to get back to sleep. They may also be irritable, have trouble concentrating, and experience other neurologic and psychological symptoms.

Patients with analgesic rebound who have tried to stop overusing pain relievers know that their headaches usually worsen before they get better. Their headaches may intensify within 4 to 6 hours after stopping the medication, becoming most intense within 1 to 2 days. This withdrawal period may last for 2 to 3 weeks. Withdrawal symptoms can sometimes be eased by the use of steroids, triptans, or nonsteroidal anti-inflammatory medications as a bridge to get through the uncomfortable period. After gradually stopping their use of analgesics, most patients notice an improvement in their headache symptoms and in their general sense of well-being within 2 to 3 weeks and more so within 2 to 3 months. They note that their headaches are less frequent and less severe. They feel better, sleep better, and are less depressed, and worry less about getting headaches.

Once overuse of pain relievers is under control, patients find that they respond to daily preventive medications, such as β-blockers, calcium blockers, antidepressants, and anti-seizure medications, as well as to migraine-specific medications such as triptans. Response to nondrug therapy such as biofeedback training also improves. None of these treatments are effective during analgesic rebound headache.

HOW TO RECOGNIZE REBOUND HEADACHE

A typical rebound headache lasts between 4 and 24 hours. The pain is mild to moderate, dull, nonthrobbing, and steady.

It can occur in any part of or all over the head, and is usually felt on both sides of the head rather than on one side. Very frequently, rebound headaches occur with a great deal of neck pain or discomfort. In most cases patients do not experience frequent migraine-type symptoms, such as throbbing, nausea, increased sensitivity to light and sound, or pain worsening with mild exertion. Sometimes, however, rebound headache does intensify into a severe migraine episode.

ERGOTAMINE REBOUND HEADACHE

Although ergotamine tartrate is effective in relieving acute migraine, its overuse results in an ergotamine rebound syndrome. Because it relieves migraine headache quickly when it works, patients with rebound are often tempted to use ergotamine for each headache, even mild ones, and they soon find that their ergotamine-responsive headaches occur more frequently. Ergotamine rebound can occur with use as infrequent as 2 days per week. Therefore, we limit our patients to 1 to 2 days per week of using Cafergot-type medications.

CAFFEINE REBOUND HEADACHE

Many headache preparations contain caffeine, a blood vessel constrictor that, when combined with analgesics, boosts headache relief. Caffeine can produce headache both when overused on a regular basis and when it is stopped abruptly (see Chapter 4).

At The New England Center for Headache in Stamford, CT, patients are questioned carefully about their caffeine intake. If it is high—over 100 to 300 mg per day, equivalent to about one to three cups of coffee—we ask them to reduce their coffee consumption slowly by one cup per week over a period of 2 to 3 weeks to avoid worsening of their headaches. Remember that a mug can be the same as two to three cups depending on its size! Patients who abstain from caffeine for a month or two can resume drinking one cup of regular coffee per day and as much decaffeinated coffee as they like without bad results.

TREATMENT OF REBOUND SYNDROMES

Treatment of rebound syndromes begins with a careful assessment of exactly what the patient is doing and a prescription for appropriate medication and a behavioral wellness program. Patients should be given a detailed explanation of the syndrome, help in withdrawing from the overused medications, and tips on avoiding the syndrome in the future. Biofeedback training and relaxation techniques can be helpful, particularly when incorporated in a comprehensive behavioral program.

The key to treatment is to discontinue the overused medications and to break the cycle of daily headache. Off-the-shelf medication can be withdrawn gradually over a few days, but prescription medications should be discontinued more slowly. Medications such as narcotics (opiates), butalbital-containing medications (such as Fiorinal), and caffeine-containing medications should be reduced over a period of several weeks. Patients using large amounts of barbiturates, narcotics, or ergotamine for a significant period of time may require hospitalization to enable them to receive effective doses of medication to prevent a severe worsening of headache and other symptoms as they withdraw from the offending medication. Outpatients should have frequent office visits until withdrawal has been completed and improvement begins. They may need to take time off from work or have help around the house till they improve.

The most effective in-hospital treatment is the administration of intravenous dihydroergotamine (DHE 45), to which intravenous steroids, antinausea medications, and valproate sodium (Depacon) may be added. Several other intravenous medications can also be used. After detoxification is complete, appropriate combinations of preventive medication can be prescribed. Then triptans are usually resumed in appropriate amounts for severe headaches.

Detoxification does not mean that one cannot use medications for occasional bad migraine attacks. The triptans can be used up to 2 to 3 days per week for migraine without causing rebound.

The follow-up behavioral wellness program should include self-help techniques, dietary instruction, an exercise and fitness program, and appropriate counseling.

NONHEADACHE DRUGS THAT MAY CAUSE HEADACHE

Some nonheadache medications used for other conditions can cause headache. Indomethacin (Indocin), a potent nonsteroidal anti-inflammatory medication, is very effective in some headache syndromes. Some patients who take it for nonheadache reasons may develop excruciating headaches, which often send them to an emergency room for evaluation. Once a serious problem has been ruled out and indomethacin has been discontinued, the headache promptly resolves.

Nifedipine (Procardia), an effective calcium channel blocker used to treat high blood pressure by dilating blood vessels, may induce a severe throbbing headache—even in nonheadache patients. A similar headache may occur in patients who take nitroglycerin for chest pain. Some blood pressure–lowering medications contain nitrates, which dilate blood vessels and cause headache. Sildenafil citrate (Viagra), used by men for impotence, dilates blood vessels and can cause headache. Vitamin A and tetracycline in large doses can sometimes cause headache. Women who take estrogen cyclically notice headache when they stop their estrogen. Some women have an increase in headache when they start to take the birth control pill. Some of the new medications that stop heartburn and ulcers, the proton pump inhibitors, can induce headache. Finally, some of the newer selective serotonin reuptake inhibitor antidepressants, such as Paxil (paroxetine hydrochloride), Prozac (fluoxetine hydrochloride), and Zoloft (sertraline hydrochloride), can occasionally increase migraine.

CHAPTER 9

ACUTE TREATMENT OF ATTACKS WITH MEDICATION

At The New England Center for Headache, in Stamford, CT, patients are treated with both pharmacologic and non-pharmacologic methods (as described in Chapter 12). Our philosophy is to use as few medications as possible for the shortest feasible period of time.

Overuse of medication designed to treat acute headache can lead to rebound syndromes and dependency. Our major concern is with the number of days per week that patients take the acute care medication, rather than the amount taken on any given day. We limit use of medication to a maximum of 2 to 3 days per week since even small amounts taken daily may induce analgesic rebound headache. Sometimes it is beneficial to take two different types of medication for 2 or 3 days each, rather than 6 days a week of just one type.

Each patient's medication program is based on that individual's needs. All patients, however, are asked to accurately record on a headache calendar how much medication they use on a daily basis (see Chapter 12).

Headache medication falls into the following three categories:

1. Symptomatic treatment. Medications in this category are directed at symptoms such as pain, nausea, or vomiting; they may also help patients to relax and possibly sleep.
2. Specific treatment. Medications in this category interfere with the process that causes the headache, thereby stopping pain and its associated symptoms such as nausea, vomiting, and sensitivity to light and sound.
3. Preventive (prophylactic) treatment. Medications in this category are taken daily to reduce or prevent frequently occurring headache. They may also be prescribed for patients who experience three or more migraine attacks per month and who have not experienced adequate

relief from specific medication. Additionally, they are used when specific medications have to be avoided, as when patients have heart disease or high blood pressure. The beneficial effects of these medications are usually not evident for 3 to 6 weeks and only at proper doses. Patients should not discontinue such medications without medical advice since stopping them abruptly could result in serious side effects or an increase in headache.

Warning: All medications have side effects. Patients should understand the desired effects of medications, how they work, and the side effects that may occur. Whenever we prescribe medication, we give our patients a list of side effects so that they can watch out for them. To avoid side effects, we start medications at low dosages and build up slowly to the optimal dosage.

DECIDING ON TREATMENT: STRATIFICATION OF CARE

Many health care providers believe that it is always best to start with gentle inexpensive symptomatic medication for headaches, and to prescribe more specific medication only when the lower-level treatment has failed. This is referred to as *step care* because the patient has to step from lower-rung treatments up to specific treatment after failure. Giving lower-level treatment first makes sense only if the patient has not tried low-end treatment already, and most people going to a doctor for headache have tried a variety of symptomatic treatments, both over the counter and prescription, without success.

The other approach for selecting medication is called *stratified care*, which is the matching of the type of treatment to the patient or headache characteristics. One way to do this is to ask how bad the headache attacks are; how quickly they get bad; whether there is nausea, vomiting, or sensitivity to light, noise, and movement; and if the headache impacts on the patient's activities of daily living. If a patient has quick onset of severe pain with vomiting, then migraine-specific medication, probably in an injection form, is appropriate. It would not make sense to prescribe a nonspecific symptomatic medication to someone so disabled.

Another approach, championed by Professor Richard Lipton, professor of neurology and public health at Albert Einstein School of Medicine in the Bronx, NY, is to ask how much lost time is caused by the headaches. In this approach to stratified care, the time loss serves as a marker for the severity of the headache. Lipton has shown in a scientific study comparing step care to stratified care that using a migraine-specific medication such as a triptan from the beginning of treatment of someone with more than 10 days of some time loss from their migraines over 3 months works better than starting with low-end medication and working up.

HOW TO EVALUATE THE SEVERITY OF MIGRAINE

If you have moderate to severe migraine attacks that produce disability, it has been shown that treating with a triptan first, instead of starting with one low-end medication after another, is more reasonable because it saves you time and money in the long run. Before initiating treatment of your migraine, consider two issues: first, how bad your headaches are and, second, how much time you are losing from them. Ask yourself how severe the headaches are at their peak intensity, how quickly they reach peak intensity, whether you have nausea and vomiting, and how quickly you develop the nausea and vomiting.

Doctors and other health care providers primarily evaluate headache using intensity of headache pain, headache frequency, and presence of nonheadache symptoms, such as nausea; sensitivity to light, sound, and movement; fatigue; and lethargy. Additionally, some patients are asked to keep headache calendars or diaries, which help them to identify triggers to migraine and to track headache frequency.

However, this type of information does not assess the impact headaches have on your life. Headaches vary among patients, and the impact of migraine may be severely disabling in many patients. Disabling migraines affect work attendance, work quality, household and family responsibilities, and leisure and social activities. Therefore, consideration of the effect headaches have on your life is critical in designing a treatment plan to reduce migraine disability.

Several tools for measuring the impact of migraine have been developed. The Migraine Disability Assessment Scale (MIDAS) was developed by Dr. Lipton, in New York, with Dr. Walter Stewart, a professor of epidemiology at the Johns Hopkins Medical School in Maryland. This questionnaire measures how migraine affects work, home, school, and recreational activities (Figure 9-1).

The following are some distinct benefits of using MIDAS:
- It is easy to use as you can complete the questionnaire independently in just a few minutes.
- It is meaningful since disability is measured as days lost in a 3-month period.
- It is valid and reliable.
- It improves communication between you and your physician.
- It improves the understanding of the burden of migraine.
- It helps identify treatment need.
- It establishes how much time you are losing to migraine.

The MIDAS questionnaire can be summarized as a way to determine how many days in the past 3 months you have operated at 50% or less capacity at work, school, home, and social and recreational activities. If the total is 11 days or more, you have moderate to high treatment need or moderate

MIDAS QUESTIONNAIRE

INSTRUCTIONS: Please answer the following questions about ALL your headaches you have had over the last 3 months.

Write your answer in the box next to each question. Write zero if you did not do the activity in the last 3 months.

DAYS

1   On how many days in the last 3 months did you miss work or school because of your headaches?

2   How many days in the last 3 months was your productivity at work or school reduced by half or more because of your headaches? (Do not include days you counted in question 1 where you missed work or school.)

3   On how many days in the last 3 months did you not do household work because of your headaches?

4   How many days in the last 3 months was your productivity in household work reduced by half or more because of your headaches? (Do not include days you counted in question 3 where you did not do household work.)

5   On how many days in the last 3 months did you miss family, social or leisure activities because of your headaches?

Total

A.   On how many days in the last 3 months did you have a headache? (If a headache lasted more than 1 day, count each day.)

B.   On a scale of 0–10, on average how painful were these headaches? (Where 0 = no pain at all, and 10 = pain as bad as it can be)

© Innovative Medical Research 1997

Once you have filled in the questionnaire, add up the total number of days from questions 1–5 (ignore A and B).

Score range	Description	Grade
0 to 5	Little or infrequent disability	Grade I
6 to 10	Mild or infrequent disability	Grade II
11 to 20	Moderate disability	Grade III
>21	Severe disability	Grade IV

Figure 9-1   The MIDAS questionnaire. (Reproduced with permission from Innovative Medical Research.)

to high disability and should probably use triptans as a first medication in treating your acute migraine attacks.

A second test for evaluating the effect of migraine on a person is the Headache Impact Test (HIT). HIT uses a computer test available on the Internet at <www.amIhealthy. com> and <www.headachetest.com> to describe the impact and severity of your headaches. You can go to the Web site, take the test, and then download and print the results for your doctor. HIT is now available as a paper tool as well—the HIT-6 (Figure 9-2).

OPTIONS FOR ACUTE TREATMENT OF LOW-LEVEL MIGRAINE

If you have low treatment need for your headache, that is if you have less than 11 days of at least 50% time loss in the past 3 months, simple or combined analgesics may work on your headache.

Option 1: Simple Analgesics

If caught early in its course, a low-level acute migraine attack can be treated in much the same way as an episodic tension-type headache, with single-agent analgesics such as ASA (Aspirin), acetaminophen (Tylenol), ibuprofen (Motrin, Advil), ketoprofen (Orudis KT), or naproxen sodium (Aleve).

Option 2: Combination Analgesics

If you have low treatment need, and single-agent analgesics are not effective, combination medications that contain ASA, acetaminophen, and caffeine (Excedrin Migraine, Anacin) can be tried. If a caffeine-containing combination product is not available, try drinking a cup of coffee (which contains 50–100 mg of caffeine) to constrict blood vessels and enhance the pain-relieving effect of the analgesic.

Option 3: Stronger Combination Medications

For attacks of low treatment need that fail options 1 and 2, treatment is the same as for episodic tension–type headache.

HIT-6™
(VERSION 1.0)

This questionnaire was designed to help you describe and communicate the way you feel and what you cannot do because of headaches.
To complete, please circle one answer for each question.

HEADACHE
IMPACT TEST™

1 When you have headaches, how often is the pain severe?

| Never | Rarely | Sometimes | Very Often | Always |

2 How often do headaches limit your ability to do usual daily activities including household work, work, school, or social activities?

| Never | Rarely | Sometimes | Very Often | Always |

3 When you have a headache, how often do you wish you could lie down?

| Never | Rarely | Sometimes | Very Often | Always |

4 In the past 4 weeks, how often have you felt too tired to do work or daily activities because of your headaches?

| Never | Rarely | Sometimes | Very Often | Always |

5 In the past 4 weeks, how often have you felt fed up or irritated because of your headaches?

| Never | Rarely | Sometimes | Very Often | Always |

6 In the past 4 weeks, how often did headaches limit your ability to concentrate on work or daily activities?

| Never | Rarely | Sometimes | Very Often | Always |

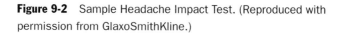

| COLUMN 1 | + | COLUMN 2 | + | COLUMN 3 | + | COLUMN 4 | + | COLUMN 5 |
| (6 points each) | | (8 points each) | | (10 points each) | | (11 points each) | | (13 points each) |

To score, add points for answers in each column. **Total Score** [   ]

Please share your HIT-6 results with your doctor.

Higher scores indicate greater impact on your life.

Score range is 36-78.

Figure 9-2 Sample Headache Impact Test. (Reproduced with permission from GlaxoSmithKline.)

Nonsteroidal anti-inflammatory drugs (NSAIDs), Midrin, or butalbital-containing medications (Fiorinal, Fioricet, Esgic) may be helpful. Remember that these lower-level treatments should only be used for low-level migraines, and that if you have moderate to severe migraines, you might get a better effect with more potent migraine-specific treatment such as a triptan. Also, triptans usually work if lower-level treatment does not work for low-level migraine because in migraine patients the low-level headaches are probably low-intensity migraines that resemble tension-type headaches but behave like migraine in terms of response to treatment.

MIGRAINE-SPECIFIC TREATMENT

Triptans

The introduction of sumatriptan (Imitrex in North America/ Inigran in Europe) in the early 1990s represented the most significant advance in migraine therapy of all time. Sumatriptan rapidly terminates a migraine attack while eliminating associated symptoms such as nausea, vomiting, and light and sound sensitivity. It is associated with minimal side effects, has brought relief to millions of migraine sufferers worldwide, and has greatly enhanced their quality of life due to its effectiveness and rapid restoration of ability to function. Sumatriptan has, in effect, become the standard against which newer antimigraine drugs are measured.

As a result of sumatriptan's resounding success, several other pharmaceutical companies have developed newer triptans in the hope of offering alternatives for people who do not receive optimal results from sumatriptan.

As a class, the triptans constrict blood vessels in the head and reverse inflammation around blood vessels in the meninges (the brain covering). They may, however, constrict other blood vessels on occasion and thus should not be given to patients with coronary artery disease, stroke, other blood vessel or vascular disease, uncontrolled high blood pressure, and two rare forms of migraine known as *hemiplegic migraine*

(migraine with paralysis on one side) and *basilar artery migraine* (associated with poor coordination and fainting).

Those patients with several risk factors for coronary disease (men over 40 years, women past menopause, obese patients, patients with high cholesterol or high blood pressure, diabetics, smokers, or those with a family history of coronary disease in a close relative at an early age) should consult with their doctor as to the safety of using triptans. The doctor may do tests and even administer these agents for the first time in the office. Blood pressure may be measured and an electrocardiogram performed prior to and following administration, in addition to monitoring for side effects. Any patient reporting chest pain or pressure should be carefully evaluated before continuing to use these drugs, although usually these are benign side effects. ***Properly prescribed*** for appropriate patients with migraine, the triptans are safe and effective.

Side effects of the triptans are generally mild and short lived and include a tingling sensation in the fingers, warmth, flushing, chest and/or neck pressure, dizziness, and rarely chest pain (Table 9-1). Patients who experience lightheadedness and fatigue should rest for a short time after dosing. Triptan side effects can be reduced by taking the medication early in a migraine attack, when the pain is mild. Also, many people adjust to the side effects, infrequent as they are, and tell us that they lessen with time.

Although these medications may eliminate the attack, the headache may return within 24 hours with sufficient severity to require a repeat dose. In reporting the usefulness of these medications to your doctor, you should include the following information:

- How long it takes before you feel the drug beginning to work
- How much time passes before you feel significant relief and can return to your usual activities

Table 9-1 Potential Triptan Side Effects	
Nuisance	Tingling of hand and fingers
	Flushing
	Warmth
	Chest and neck pressure
	Drowsiness or dizziness
Important to tell your doctor	Chest pain

- How much better the pain is, for example, there is a 100% improvement (pain free)
- The percentage of the time the drug works, for example, 9 of 10 times
- The percentage of attacks in which the headache returns within 24 hours
- How many of your attacks are treated with a single dose of medication and no further medication of any kind
- If the headache recurs, how long it takes to return

As with any medication prescribed by your doctor, triptans should be taken only as directed. Maintaining good control of migraine can help reduce the need for emergency department and physician visits, and may improve overall quality of life.

A brief review of information available for each of these medicines follows (Table 9-2). Since several effective triptan medications are available in a variety of delivery systems (tablets, injections, nasal sprays, and preparations that dissolve instantly on your tongue without the need for water), do not lose hope if you do not respond to one preparation or have uncomfortable side effects; you may do well with a different triptan—or even the same one—for your next attack.

Table 9-2 Description of the Triptans

Generic Name	Brand Name	Form	Dose (mg)	Maximum in 24 Hr (mg)	Quantity in Box
Group I					
Sumatriptan	Imitrex	Subcutaneous injection	6	12	2
		Tablet	25, 50, 100 (50 is best starting dose)	200	9
		Nasal spray	5, 20 (20 is best starting dose)	40	6
Zolmitriptan	Zomig	Tablet	2.5, 5	10	6 (2.5 mg), 3 (5 mg)
	Zomig ZMT	Melt	2.5, 5	10	6 (2.5 mg), 3 (5 mg)
	Zomig	Nasal spray	5	Unknown	Unknown
Rizatriptan	Maxalt	Tablet, melt	5, 10 (10 is best dose; 5 if on propranolol)	30 (15 if on propranolol)	6
Almotriptan	Axert	Tablet	12.5	25	6
Eletriptan	Relpax	Tablet	Unknown	Unknown	Unknown
Group II					
Naratriptan	Amerge	Tablet	1, 2.5	5	9
Frovatriptan	Frova	Tablet	2.5	7.5	9

Types of triptans. Triptans can be divided into two groups: group I, the fast-acting higher-powered oral triptans; and group II, the slower-onset lower-powered triptans, with possibly lower recurrence.

The group I triptans includes sumatriptan (Imitrex), zolmitriptan (Zomig), rizatriptan (Maxalt), almotriptan (Axert), and eletriptan (Relpax). Only eletriptan is not yet marketed in the United States at the time of this publication.

Sumatriptan (Imitrex/Imigran) is available in three dosage forms: injection, tablets, and nasal spray. Each injection delivers 6 mg via an autoinjector, called a Statdose pen; this is the most rapidly acting form. Injection can be repeated once if the headache returns with sufficient severity. Maximum dose is two injections in 24 hours. Seventy percent of the time, patients feel relief within 1 hour, and over 80% of the time, within 2 hours. The chance of a headache coming back (recurrence) within 24 hours is 30 to 40%, with an average time to recurrence of 14 hours.

In a study conducted by our group at The New England Center for Headache in Stamford, CT, and published in the journal *Headache*, we reported an 84% success rate in the first 100 patients who tried this medication in the injectable form. Eighty-one percent of the patients said it worked better than anything they had tried previously for migraine, and many termed it "a miracle drug." Forty-six percent of our patients had a recurrent headache between 8 and 15 hours after the first dose; this was treated effectively with a second dose. No patient stopped using the drug because of side effects.

Sumatriptan is available in the United States and Canada in a tablet form at 25, 50, and 100 mg doses. Maximum dosage is 200 mg in 24 hours. About 61% of people experience pain relief by 2 hours with the 50 mg pill, and almost 80% by 4 hours. The best starting dose is 50 mg. The 100 mg tablet is useful for patients who do not completely eliminate their pain with 50 mg, or in whom the migraine recurs. It shows maximal benefit when taken early in an attack.

Sumatriptan nasal spray is available in 5 and 20 mg single-dose units; dosage is one spray in one nostril. Most patients will respond to the 20 mg dose, which works faster than a tablet. We recommend spraying it in one nostril with the head in a neutral position or bent slightly forward, and pointing the tip of the sprayer up and in. When you spray it, do not sniff it in to the back of your throat—try to keep it in your nose. Taste disturbance (often described as a "bad taste") is the most common side effect, followed by nausea, vomiting, fatigue, and flushing.

The advantage of sumatriptan is that you can switch from one form to another in the same day. For example, if you vomit or the pill fails to work, you can use the shot.

Zolmitriptan (Zomig) is available in tablet form in 2.5 and 5 mg. Zomig ZMT 2.5 and 5 mg forms are available as rapidly dissolving orange-flavored pills or melt tablets that are placed on the tongue. Up to 67% of patients achieve pain relief in 2 hours with the 2.5 mg pill. It is safe to take 2.5 or 5 mg to treat the initial migraine and to use either 2.5 or 5 mg at 2 hours if the migraine persists. With one to two doses, people who respond to zolmitriptan are able to successfully treat 95% of attacks over a year, a very high consistency. The 5 mg zolmitriptan is more likely to make a patient pain free than is the 2.5 mg dose, and it is used as a starting dose for many patients.

The orange-flavored Zomig ZMT, and melting orally dissolvable tablets in general, are designed to encourage patients to take the medication early in an attack because of the convenience of the melt formulation. Orally dissolvable tablets are not absorbed in the mouth or under the tongue; they dissolve in the saliva and go through the gastrointestinal (GI) tract where they are absorbed in the small intestine. But because they do not need to be taken with liquid, which can trigger or worsen nausea for some, many patients take them earlier in an attack and find them more convenient than and preferable to conventional tablets.

Zolmitriptan works well in all migraine types, including migraines occurring around menses and migraine present on awakening. As noted above, all of the triptans must be used cautiously in patients with cardiovascular risk factors. The most common side effects of zolmitriptan are nausea, dizziness, sleepiness, and tingling in the fingers; these effects are infrequent, mild, and transient. Recurrence rate for zolmitriptan is about 30%. A fast-acting nasal spray is likely to be available in 2003. In the United States, the maximum amount of zolmitriptan that you should take in 24 hours is 10 mg.

Rizatriptan (Maxalt) is a fast-onset triptan and comes in 5 and 10 mg pills and rapidly dissolving tablets (Maxalt MLT—mint-flavored melts). Over 70% of attacks are relieved with the 10 mg dose in 2 hours, and many studies have found that rizatriptan is a very rapidly active oral triptan. The maximum amount that you should take in 24 hours is 30 mg.

For most patients, 10 mg rizatriptan works better than does 5 mg and is the proper starting dose. There is some evidence that, for treating migraines that have reached a moderate to severe intensity, rizatriptan is the most likely oral triptan to be successfully treated with a single tablet.

If you are taking propranolol (Inderal) for migraine prevention or other reasons such as high blood pressure, you need to use the 5 mg dose of rizatriptan. In that case the maximum amount that you can take in 24 hours is 15 mg.

Almotriptan (Axert) is available in a dose of 12.5 mg. Pain relief at 2 hours occurs in about 61%, similar to relief with sumatriptan tablets, and its recurrence rate is identical to that with sumatriptan. However, almotriptan is different from sumatriptan in that it shows slightly fewer nuisance side effects, so some patients tolerate it better than other group I oral triptans. The maximum dose per 24 hours is 25 mg.

Eletriptan (Relpax) is not available in the United States and Canada at the time of this writing. It is currently marketed in Europe and expected in the United States in 2003.

Group II triptans, naratriptan (Amerge) and frovatriptan (Frova), are slower-onset triptans. Naratriptan is available as 1 mg and 2.5 mg tablets. It should be used in different headaches from those treated with sumatriptan, zolmitriptan, rizatriptan, and almotriptan. These latter four triptans are fast acting, can be used at almost any time in the headache, and have a recurrence rate of 30 to 40%. Naratriptan is slower in its onset, with 66% of people obtaining headache relief at 4 hours. (In general the triptans of group II take twice as long as the group I triptans to take effect.) However, if you take naratriptan early in a migraine (in the first 90 minutes), recurrence can be low or even zero, and it may be more effective than when taken late in a migraine. When directly compared with sumatriptan and rizatriptan, naratriptan is associated with a lower likelihood of the treated migraine recurring.

In addition, the side effects of naratriptan are so minimal, it is difficult to tell its effects from those of a sugar pill (placebo). It is referred to as *the gentle triptan* because of its low nuisance side effects. However, as with all triptans, it cannot be used by people with vascular disease.

Consequently, naratriptan is a good choice if you are sensitive to medications, develop your migraines slowly over hours, have long-duration or menstrual migraine, or do not wake up with a migraine. The maximum amount you should take in 24 hours is 5 mg.

Frovatriptan (Frova) is available as a 2.5 mg tablet with a slow onset of action, similar to that of naratriptan, and a 2-hour likelihood of pain relief of 36 to 46% that increases to 60% at 4 hours. Thus, as with naratriptan, it takes about twice as long as do group I triptans to take effect. It may be a good medication to try in long-duration or slow-onset attacks, or menstrual migraine.

Although one study found no difference in the recurrence rate of frovatriptan in direct comparison with sumatriptan, in many other studies, the recurrence rates with frovatriptan were very low, in the teens and even below 10% in one study. The other special attribute of the drug was noticed in one study in which people were given frovatriptan to use over a year. It was found that the one-third of patients who achieved headache relief at 2 hours maintained this quick response over the entire year, coupled with a very low (6%) likelihood of the headache recurring. Thus, frovatriptan may be a useful medication for the subset of people who demonstrate both the quick headache relief and the remarkably low recurrence rate.

Summary.   Because of the importance of the triptans in treating the acute migraine attack, it is worth summarizing how each one has its own characteristic place in treatment of an individual. Sumatriptan has the highest potency (injection), quickest onset (injection and nasal spray), and greatest flexibility of form. Zolmitriptan has the highest consistency over time and is available as a conventional tablet, and the easy-to-use ZMT or melt form is likely to be used earlier in an attack. Rizatriptan has a slightly quicker onset of effect than have the other available oral triptans, with the greatest likelihood of one tablet terminating a moderate to severe attack. Almotriptan has the effectiveness of oral sumatriptan, with a slightly more favorable side effect profile. Naratriptan has the gentlest nuisance side effect profile of them all, and the lowest recurrence rate. Frovatriptan treats a subset of people with consistently quick headache relief and very low recurrence, and shows a producing low recurrence rate. Remember that triptans should not be taken if you have heart disease or untreated high blood pressure or have had a stroke or any type of blood vessel problems.

The best triptan for you is the one that works. A failure to respond to one triptan does not predict a failure to respond to another; nor do side effects from one predict side effects from another.

Ergots

Ergotamine tartrate (Cafergot) has been in use for over 50 years as a specific migraine agent. The rectal suppositories are better absorbed and more effective than are ergotamine tablets in the treatment of headache.

We recommend one to two ergotamine tablets be taken at the start of a migraine attack, followed by one more tablet in an hour if needed. Ergotamine works best in a non-nauseating dose; if you cannot tolerate a full coated tablet, you should use a suppository. Initially use one-quarter of the suppository and repeat in an hour if needed. Most patients need to pretreat with an antinausea medication before use of either form of ergotamine. Refer to antinauseants for recommendations about pretreatment to prevent nausea. We instruct patients to use ergotamine preferably only 1 day per week, and no more than 2 days per week. The only exceptions are for women who may need to use it for 3 or 4 consecutive days during menstrual periods, and for cluster patients, who may need to use it more frequently.

Side effects of ergotamine include nausea, vomiting, and diarrhea, and some patients experience tingling in the fingers and toes, chest pain, and muscle cramps.

Dihydroergotamine

Dihydroergotamine (DHE 45) is chemically related to ergotamine tartrate but is more effective and less likely to cause nausea. Originally available only as an injectable solution, it is also available in the nasal spray form Migranal.

The initial injectable dose is 1 mg, which may be repeated in 2 hours if needed. The headache is not likely to recur once it disappears. When given intravenously the dose should be lower to start—0.25 or 0.5 mg—and always preceded by an antinausea medication. For the nasal spray, we recommend one spray in each nostril as an initial dose, to be repeated in 15 minutes. These four sprays contain 0.5 mg each for a total dose of 2 mg. DHE 45 is less likely to cause recurrent or rebound headache than is ergotamine and can be used several days per week.

The most frequent side effects from the DHE 45 nasal spray are occasional stuffiness of the nose, muscle cramps, and diarrhea.

Warning: Patients who take macrolide antibiotics (erythromycin, azithromycin [Zithromax], and clarithromycin [Biaxin]) and/or have coronary artery disease, untreated hypertension, or peripheral vascular disease, or who could be pregnant, should not take DHE or ergotamine. All the precautions that apply to triptans also apply to ergots.

Treatment for People Who Cannot Take Triptans

For those with vascular disease, or those types of migraine for which the US Food and Drug Administration prohibits the use of triptans (basilar artery and hemiplegic migraines, see above), we prescribe a medication that does not affect blood vessels strongly, such as an NSAID in prescription-strength doses, or a combination medication. Midrin contains isometheptene, which only very mildly constricts blood vessels, combined with acetaminophen to relieve pain and dichloralphenazone, which is a mild tranquilizer. Fiorinal contains a barbiturate (butalbital), a pain reliever (ASA), and caffeine.

Prescription NSAIDs can be helpful in treating a tension-type headache, a mild migraine, and occasionally a significant migraine, especially in those who cannot take a triptan. Refer to Table 9-3 for a listing of NSAIDs. Prescription NSAIDs may work better than those available off the shelf. At The New England Center for Headache, we usually prescribe the following: naproxen sodium (Anaprox), ketoprofen (Orudis), meclofenamate (Meclomen), and flurbiprofen (Ansaid).

The standard dose for prescription NSAIDs is two tablets or capsules initially followed by two more in 1 hour if necessary, with a maximum of four per day, 3 days per week. NSAIDs should be taken with food. Patients taking NSAIDs may experience stomach pain, heartburn, kidney problems, elevated blood pressure, and GI bleeding (watch for dark or tarry stools) and sometimes eye problems and occasional drowsiness (with use of indomethacin).

Recently, rofecoxib (Vioxx) 12.5, 25, and 50 mg, celecoxib (Celebrex) 100 and 200 mg, and valdecoxib (Bextra) 10 or 20 mg have become available. They appear to cause fewer GI problems than do traditional NSAIDs, and they appear to be effective in many types of headache. These newer NSAIDs are taken only once per day. Recently, valdecoxib has been described as causing rare but life-threatening skin allergic reactions.

The dose of the combination medicine Midrin is one or two capsules at the start of a headache, followed by one or two more in 1 hour if the headache persists. Patients should take no more than five capsules in a day, and use of Midrin should be limited to 3 days per week. Side effects of Midrin include occasional dizziness, drowsiness, or GI symptoms. Midrin may be effective early in a mild migraine attack, and it has so few side effects that we prescribe it on occasion for older children.

Warning: Dangerous drug interactions can occur if Midrin is taken with a monoamine oxidase inhibitor (MAOI) antidepressant (see page 82) such as phenelzine (Nardil) or tranylcypromine (Parnate).

Table 9-3 Nonsteroidal Anti-inflammatory Drugs Commonly Used in Migraine and Tension-Type Headache

Generic Name	Brand Names	Dose (mg)	Side Effects	Comments
Naproxen	Naprosyn	250, 375, 500	Can cause stomach ulcers, kidney problems, elevated blood pressure, and excessive bleeding	
Naproxen sodium	Anaprox Naprelan Aleve	275, 550 375, 500 220	See above	
Diclofenac	Cataflam Voltaren Voltaren-XR	25, 50, 75, 100	See above	
Indomethacin	Indocin Indocin SR	25, 50 75	See above, plus eye problems and occasional drowsiness	
Etodolac	Lodine Lodine XL	200, 300, 400 400, 500, 600	Can cause stomach ulcers, kidney problems, elevated blood pressure, and excessive bleeding	
Ibuprofen	Advil Motrin	200 400, 600, 800	See above	
Fenoprofen	Nalfon	200, 300	See above	
Ketoprofen	Orudis KT Orudis Oruvail	12.5 25, 50, 75 100, 150, 200	See above	
Flurbiprofen	Ansaid	100	See above	
Mefenamic acid	Ponstel	250	See above	
Nabumetone	Relafen	500, 750	See above	
Meclofenamate	Meclomen	100, 200	See above	
Ketorolac	Toradol	10 mg pill, 30 or 60 mg ampoule for injection	See above, plus higher incidence of ulcers	
Rofecoxib	Vioxx	12.5, 25, 50	See above, but lower incidence of stomach problems	A new, cyclo-oxygenase 2 (Cox-2) inhibitor
Celecoxib	Celebrex	100, 200	See above, but lower incidence of stomach problems	A new, cyclo-oxygenase 2 (Cox-2) inhibitor

Continued

Table 9-3 Continued

Generic Name	Brand Names	Dose (mg)	Side Effects	Comments
Valdecoxib	Bextra	10, 20	See above, but lower incidence of stomach problems; also reported to cause severe allergic reactions	A new cyclooxygenase-2 (Cox-2) inhibitor

If the NSAIDs or Midrin do not provide adequate relief, we sometimes prescribe medications that contain the short-acting barbiturate butalbital. Refer to Table 9-4 for the names, ingredients, and recommended doses of butalbital-containing medications. If used frequently, any of these medications can cause dependence and rebound headache. Those that contain acetaminophen instead of ASA are easier on the stomach but tougher on the liver; combinations that contain codeine are more potent pain relievers, but they are more likely to produce dependency.

One or two tablets of butalbital-containing medications are the initial dose, and one or two more tablets may be taken 4 hours later if necessary. Exceeding the daily limits listed in Table 9-4 may cause rebound headache, dependency,

Table 9-4 Combination Analgesics Containing Butalbital

Drug/Components	Size (mg)	Recommended Dosage
Fiorinal		1–2 tablets every 4 hours as needed;
Butalbital	50	no more than 6/day, no more
ASA	325	than 2 days/week
Caffeine	40	
Fioricet/Esgic		1–2 tablets every 4 hours as
Butalbital	50	needed; no more than 6/day,
Acetaminophen	325	no more than 2 days/week
Caffeine	40	
Phrenilin		1–2 tablets every 4 hours as
Butalbital	50	needed; no more than 6/day,
Acetaminophen	325	no more than 2 days/week

or a "drugged" feeling. Patients should limit intake to 2 to 3 days per week. Butalbital-containing medications may cause drowsiness, poor coordination, and slurred speech. **Warning:** Do not drink alcohol, drive, or operate machinery after taking medications containing butalbital.

RESCUE MEDICATIONS

When all else fails, it is sometimes necessary to take medications to dull the pain and help you to sleep. These medications are not as effective as triptans, which restore you to normal function.

Opiates

We prescribe opiates (narcotics) for our patients as back-up rescue medication only when absolutely necessary. We prefer to use gentle low-level opiates, but even these can cause drowsiness and nausea. The low-level opioids include tramadol (Ultram), propoxyphene (Darvon), codeine, and hydrocodone/acetaminophen (Vicodin). Sometimes it is necessary to prescribe stronger more sedating opiates such as oxycodone (OxyIR, Roxicodone), hydromorphone (Dilaudid), morphine (MSIR), and butorphanol tartrate (Stadol nasal spray). When appropriate we prescribe hydromorphone (Dilaudid) suppository or butorphanol tartrate nasal spray (Stadol NS) because they are easy for patients to use, even when vomiting is present, and permit home treatment of severe pain.

Drowsiness is a well-known opiate side effect, so plan to stay home after taking a dose. Since opiates may help you sleep, they are particularly useful for nighttime headaches. Other side effects include nausea, vomiting, and dizziness.

Warning: Butorphanol may inactivate other opiates. Use this medication with caution if you are taking other medications that cause drowsiness. Overuse of any opiate can cause dependency and a drugged feeling. Dosing recommendations must be followed carefully and use limited to one dose per week or less.

Antianxiety Agents

Migraine patients with anxiety may feel relief when using benzodiazepine minor tranquilizers such as lorazepam (Ativan), alprazolam (Xanax), diazepam (Valium), and clorazepate (Tranxene). Although these drugs may relieve anxiety and promote relaxation, they can cause dependency and worsen headache syndromes. Buspirone (Buspar) does not cause dependency and can be used daily for treatment of anxiety.

Steroids

Dexamethasone (Decadron), which is a steroid, can be used if all else fails. It should be used only once or twice per month because frequent use of steroids can produce serious side effects. We prescribe a single 4 mg tablet, which may be repeated in 3 hours if the first dose is not effective. Up to 70% of our patients get relief of their headache from the use of dexamethasone, even after a triptan has failed them.

Occasional use of dexamethasone may cause reddening of the face, sleeplessness, and a slight increase in blood pressure. Excessive use produces multiple side effects, including loss of bone strength, ulcers, and joint deterioration.

Warning: Patients with uncontrolled high blood pressure, diabetes, psychiatric illness, or active ulcer disease or acute infection should avoid the use of steroids.

Antinausea Medication

Migraine can cause nausea, and sometimes antinausea medications (antiemetics) must be used as rescue. Other times antinausea medication taken with antipain medication yields a better response than does either alone. Antiemetics combat nausea occurring because of migraine or as a side effect of specific medication such as ergotamine tartrate (Cafergot). Antiemetics that may help include promethazine (Phenergan), metoclopramide (Reglan), prochlorperazine (Compazine), trimethobenzamide (Tigan), chlorpromazine (Thorazine), hydroxyzine (Vistaril), and an off-the-shelf liquid preparation, Emetrol. Emetrol can be added to any of the previously mentioned antinauseants, and can be repeated every 15 to 30 minutes. The newer antinauseants, ondansetron (Zofran) and granisetron (Kytril), are also extremely effective.

The antinausea medications we prefer to prescribe are promethazine (Phenergan), taken by mouth or as a suppository, and oral metoclopramide (Reglan). Promethazine is more likely than is metoclopramide to make you drowsy and help you sleep; metoclopramide keeps you alert but can occasionally cause mild agitation. If you need to be alert so you can go to work, we recommend you use metoclopramide about 15 minutes before taking an ergotamine-type specific medication. If you prefer to sleep and can remain at home, promethazine is the preferred choice. Prochlorperazine (Compazine) may be helpful, but some patients may experience muscle spasms when using it. Of all of the traditional antinausea medications, promethazine is the most useful for rescue and sleep, and metoclopramide is the most useful to add to other medications during the day.

Ondansetron (Zofran) is a different type of antinausea medication that is helpful in treating the nausea of migraine, and it almost never causes drowsiness. It is available as a tablet, a melt, and as an intravenous injection. Granisetron (Kytril) is available as a 1 mg tablet and by IV injection.

Miscellaneous Treatments

Other medications for headache include muscle relaxants such as carisoprodol (Soma), methocarbamol (Robaxin), cyclobenzaprine hydrochloride (Flexeril), and metaxalone (Skelaxin). Diazepam (Valium) and clonazepam (Klonopin) are also used as anticonvulsants and may be beneficial for patients whose headaches are associated with neck pain, muscle spasm, and anxiety. Baclofen (Lioresal) and tizanidine (Zanaflex) are highly potent antispasticity drugs typically used in patients with cerebral palsy and multiple sclerosis. They may be helpful in some patients with tension-type headaches and muscle spasm. Tizanidine has been tested recently in patients with chronic daily headache and is helpful when sleeping is difficult.

The problem with all of these medications is that they are nonspecific, create drowsiness, and can be habituating. Patients with neck pain and headache usually have migraine and are better off using triptans than any of the long list of "muscle-relaxing" medications.

TENSION-TYPE HEADACHE VERSUS MIGRAINE: HOW TO KNOW WHICH TO TREAT

For many years, headache specialists thought that we should treat tension-type headaches one way and migraine another. Now we know that most people with migraine have a spectrum of headaches, from those similar to the tension type to those that are obviously migraine. About 75% of attacks of low-level migraine initially seem to be tension-type headache but end up being disabling migraine. It is the wrong approach to treat them with low-level or over-the-counter medications and rescue with triptans when the attacks get very bad. For this reason, we have stopped recommending treating the low-level tension-type attacks with low-level treatment; most of the attacks end up moderate to severe, and triptans work better if taken when the pain is mild. Also, if the triptan is taken later, there is a lower likelihood of becoming pain free and a greater likelihood that the headache will recur. Finally, when the triptans are taken early, the nuisance side effects are less.

So, our recommendation to patients with disabling migraines is to take the triptan early in the attack, at mild pain, and not to wait or treat with a lower-end medication first. If you become pain free with a triptan and the migraine does not recur, you will actually use fewer, not more, triptan tablets over time.

CHAPTER 10

PREVENTIVE TREATMENT OF MIGRAINE WITH MEDICATION

When two or more severe migraine attacks occur per week, and if each attack lasts for more than 24 hours or if attacks are difficult to treat with the symptomatic and specific acute care migraine medications mentioned in Chapter 9, then daily preventive medications should be taken to decrease or block migraine attacks. There are several categories of medications that can be used (Table 10-1); some patients do better with one type of medication than with another.

β-BLOCKERS

β-Blockers may work by stabilizing arteries or preventing the central generator of migraine in the brainstem from firing. Of the many β-blockers, propranolol (Inderal), atenolol (Tenormin), metoprolol (Lopressor, Toprol-XL), nadolol (Corgard), and timolol (Blocadren) are the most effective for prevention of migraine. Those we prescribe most frequently are metoprolol, atenolol, nadolol, and propranolol.

Our patients take metoprolol (Toprol-XL) 50 mg once daily, increasing to 100 mg if necessary, or propranolol 10 to 20 mg twice a day, increasing by 10 to 20 mg every 5 days up to a dose of about 60 to 120 mg. If a patient does well on short-acting propranolol in divided doses, we may then switch to the longer-acting form. Atenolol is usually started at 25 mg in the morning and can be slowly raised to 50 to 100 mg.

Potential side effects of β-blockers include fatigue, asthma, depression, impotence, reduced blood pressure and pulse rate, weight gain, reduced tolerance to physical activity, and dizziness on standing.

Warning: β-Blockers should not be given to people with asthma, diabetes, low blood sugar (hypoglycemia), slow heart rate, low blood pressure, or severe depression. They should also

Table 10-1 Preventive Treatment of Migraine

Generic Name	Trade Name	Dosage Range (mg/day)	Side Effects
β-Blockers			
Propranolol	Inderal	20–360	Fatigue, depression, weight gain, asthma, impotence, reduced blood pressure and pulse rate, dizziness, reduced tolerance to physical activity, cold hands *NOT for use by diabetics or asthmatics*
Metoprolol	Toprol-XL, Lopressor	50–100	Fatigue, depression, weight gain, asthma, impotence, reduced blood pressure and pulse rate, dizziness, reduced tolerance to physical activity, cold hands *NOT for use by diabetics or asthmatics*
Nadolol	Corgard	20–160	Fatigue, depression, weight gain, asthma, impotence, reduced blood pressure and pulse rate, dizziness, reduced tolerance to physical activity, cold hands *NOT for use by diabetics or asthmatics*
Timolol	Blocadren	10–40	Fatigue, depression, weight gain, asthma, impotence, reduced blood pressure and pulse rate, dizziness, reduced tolerance to physical activity, cold hands *NOT for use by diabetics or asthmatics*
Atenolol	Tenormin	25–100	Fatigue, depression, weight gain, asthma, impotence, reduced blood pressure and pulse rate, dizziness, reduced tolerance to physical activity, cold hands *NOT for use by diabetics or asthmatics*

Continued

Table 10-1 Continued

Generic Name	Trade Name	Dosage Range (mg/day)	Side Effects
Calcium channel blockers			
Verapamil	Calan, Covera, Isoptin, Verelan	80–480	Reduced blood pressure and pulse rate, constipation, altered heart rhythm, foot swelling
Diltiazem	Cardizem, Tiazac	60–360	Reduced blood pressure and pulse rate, constipation, altered heart rhythm, foot swelling
Amlodipine	Norvasc	2.5–10	Reduced blood pressure and pulse rate, altered heart rhythm, foot swelling
Nisoldipine	Sular	10–40	Reduced blood pressure and pulse rate, altered heart rhythm, foot swelling
Flunarizine (available only in Canada and Europe)	Sibelium	5–10	Weight gain, depression *CAUTION with use in patients with cardiac disease*
Antidepressants See Table 10–2			
Antiepilepsy drugs			
Divalproex sodium	Depakote Depakote ER	500–1,500 500, 1,000	Drowsiness, hair loss, tremor, diarrhea, weight gain, foot swelling, inflammation of liver, bone marrow, or pancreas *NOT for use by women who are or may be pregnant*
Gabapentin	Neurontin	600–2,700	Drowsiness, dizziness, weight gain

Continued

Table 10-1 Continued

Generic Name	Trade Name	Dosage Range (mg/day)	Side Effects
Antiepilepsy drugs (*Continued*)			
Topiramate	Topamax	45–200	Weight loss, confusion, kidney stones, glaucoma, tingling of arms and legs
Tiagabine	Gabitril	8–48	Drowsiness *NOT for use in pregnancy, in people with liver disease, or in combination with barbiturates*
Serotonin 2 antagonists			
Cyproheptadine	Periactin	4–16	Drowsiness, dry mouth, constipation, weight gain
Methysergide	Sansert	4–12	Drowsiness, hallucinations, muscle aches, gastrointestinal upset *NOT to be used longer than 6 months and not to be used in people with vascular disease, inflammation in leg veins, or stomach ulcers, or in people taking triptans*
Methylergonovine	Methergine	0.2–1.2	Same as Methysergide
NSAIDS See Table 9–3			

not be used in severe cases of migraine accompanied by weakness on one side of the body or other evidence of focal brain dysfunction such as visual aura. Patients who need to stop taking β-blockers should taper the dosage gradually over several days to prevent a withdrawal reaction including a rapid heartbeat. Patients on propranolol who use the triptan rizatriptan (Maxalt) should use only a 5 mg dose of the triptan.

ANTIDEPRESSANTS

Antidepressant drugs, which increase serotonin levels, are among the best medications to treat migraine preventively. Drugs from each of the three major categories, the tricyclic antidepressants (TCAs) and tetracyclic antidepressants, the selective serotonin reuptake inhibitors (SSRIs), and the monoamine oxidase inhibitors (MAOIs), may be effective for these headaches. Antidepressants (Table 10-2) should be chosen both for their ability to increase serotonin levels and for other effects, such as drowsiness or stimulation, that may be helpful for some patients.

TCAs

Amitriptyline (Elavil) has been the gold standard for treatment of chronic headache, but its use may be limited by some of its side effects. At our center we prescribe antidepressants for patients with migraine (and also for chronic tension-type headache) as follows:

Table 10-2 Antidepressants	
Generic (Brand) Names	**Generic (Brand) Names**
TCAs	**SSRIs**
Amitriptyline (Elavil)	Citalopram (Celexa)
Doxepin (Sinequan, Adapin)	Escitalopram (Lexapro)
Nortriptyline (Pamelor, Aventyl)	Fluoxetine (Prozac)
Desipramine (Norpramin)	Fluvoxamine (Luvox)
Trazodone (Desyrel)	Sertraline (Zoloft)
Imipramine (Tofranil)	Paroxetine (Paxil)
Amoxapine (Asendin)	**Miscellaneous**
Protriptyline (Vivactil)	Bupropion (Wellbutrin)
Maprotiline (Ludiomil)	Venlafaxine (Effexor)
Clomipramine (Anafranil)	Mirtazapine (Remeron)
	Nefazodone (Serzone)
	MAOIs
	Phenelzine (Nardil)
	Isocarboxazid (Marplan)
	Tranylcypromine (Parnate)

- For patients who have trouble sleeping through the night, awaken early in the morning, and who may be depressed—amitriptyline, doxepin (Sinequan), or trazodone (Desyrel), which is neither a TCA nor an SSRI
- For patients who require less sedation—TCAs including nortriptyline (Pamelor), desipramine (Norpramin), imipramine (Tofranil), and protriptyline (Vivactil), the last two of which have the least sedating effects and can be given in the morning

Two to 4 weeks of treatment may be required before patients notice an improvement in their headaches.

Amitriptyline, nortriptyline, or doxepin are started at 10 mg, 1 to 2 hours before bedtime, and raised 10 mg every sixth night, until a total of 50 mg or five capsules or tablets is reached. This is an average dose; it may have to be adjusted up or down. All medications are started at low doses and raised gradually to avoid side effects.

All TCAs have possible side effects, the most distressing of which are increased appetite, weight gain, drowsiness in the morning, dry mouth, and constipation. Blurred vision, sexual dysfunction, and urinary hesitancy occur less frequently.

Warning: Do not use TCAs if you have heart rhythm irregularities or glaucoma, or experience difficulty urinating.

SSRIs

The most frequently prescribed SSRIs are fluoxetine (Prozac), sertraline (Zoloft), paroxetine (Paxil), and citalopram (Celexa). SSRIs tend to have fewer side effects than the TCAs and are less likely to cause drowsiness and weight gain. They work well in chronic tension-type headache but, unfortunately, are rarely effective in preventing or reducing the frequency of migraine. In some cases they can actually increase migraine.

A patient taking fluoxetine would start with 10 mg each morning for 2 weeks, after which the dose could be raised to 20 mg if no side effects occurred. Maximum benefit begins to occur between 3 and 6 weeks, and few people experience significant side effects. Higher doses may be necessary. Fluoxetine is long acting and remains in the body for days after it has been discontinued. Prozac has recently become available in a 90 mg pill that lasts for a week called Prozac Weekly.

Mild agitation or hyperactivity shortly following the morning dose is the most common side effect associated with the SSRIs; this effect usually stops occurring within 2 weeks. Insomnia, tremor, and difficulty having an orgasm or other sexual dysfunction may occur. On rare occasions SSRIs can make patients feel "off" psychologically. These drugs may cause depression or an increase in headache. Patients who notice drowsiness should take SSRIs at night. Weight loss is more common than is weight gain, though either may occur.

Warning: SSRIs should be used cautiously in severely depressed patients and must not be used with MAOIs.

MAOIs

When simpler medications have not worked, MAOIs such as phenelzine (Nardil) can be tried. Patients who take MAOIs must eliminate from their diets foods that contain tyramine to avoid drastic changes in blood pressure. The dietary restrictions are easy to follow but must be followed strictly.

Phenelzine is started with early morning doses of 15 mg, eventually building over the course of 1 month to a maximum dose of 30 mg in the morning and 30 mg at lunch time.

Insomnia, weight gain, and changes in blood pressure are the major side effects of phenelzine.

Warning: MAOIs should not be taken with Midrin, Demerol, and some other opiates, off-the-shelf cold medicines, and foods that contain tyramine (such as cheese, red wine, liver). When taking an MAOI, TCAs should be used with great caution, if at all; SSRIs and certain triptans (such as sumatripan, zolmitriptan, and rizatriptan) are not to be used.

ANTICONVULSANTS

Anticonvulsants, which are used in seizure disorders (epilepsy), are useful for prevention of migraine. Divalproex sodium (Depakote in the United States, Epival in Canada) effectively reduces the frequency of migraine in many patients and has been approved by the US Food and Drug Administration (FDA) as safe and effective in the prevention of migraine. It is also available in the United States in a convenient long-acting form, Depakote ER. Other anticonvulsants such as phenytoin (Dilantin) and carbamazepine (Tegretol) have not been as effective.

Divalproex Sodium

If started at low doses, and increased slowly over time, divalproex sodium is less likely to cause side effects. It is safer for use in adults than in young children. We have adult patients start with 125 mg of divalproex sodium once per day and slowly increase the dose until they switch to Depakote ER (extended release), which is taken in a single daily dose of 500 or 1,000 mg. Some physicians start patients on Depakote ER 500 mg at night. This form of Depakote may cause fewer side effects than the short-acting form.

At the doses necessary to treat epilepsy or manic-depressive illness, divalproex sodium may frequently cause significant side effects. At the lower doses used for preventing migraine, the side effects are far less frequent. The high-dose side effects include the breakage of hair shafts on brushing (which could lead to slight thinning of hair), drowsiness, tremor, weight gain, nausea, diarrhea, and foot swelling. Occasional blood tests should be performed to make certain that liver, pancreatic, and kidney function and complete blood count remain normal.

Warning: Women who are pregnant, or who may become pregnant, should not take divalproex sodium because it can cause serious spinal cord defects in the fetus. It

The only side effect of botulinum toxin injection is a rare droopy eyelid; this effect is dependent on where the injections are placed, and lasts only a week or two, if it occurs. Thus, the advantages of botulinum toxin injection in preventing migraine are that it does not require daily dosage and has very few side effects. In fact, botulinum toxin injection is so safe that the FDA recently approved it in the cosmetic treatment of wrinkles. The disadvantage is that it requires injections about every 3 months.

SEROTONIN 2 ANTAGONISTS

Cyproheptadine

Cyproheptadine (Periactin) is an antihistamine that blocks serotonin 2 receptors. It is somewhat effective in preventing migraine attacks in children, but less so in adults.

Cyproheptadine is available in tablets and liquid form. The starting dose is one-quarter of a 4 mg tablet (1 mg) 1 to 2 hours before bedtime; dosage can be slowly increased to a total of two to four tablets.

Children tolerate cyproheptadine well and experience few side effects. Adults, however, may become drowsy or have increased appetite with weight gain. Drowsiness may be beneficial for patients who sleep poorly. Some people with nasal problems appreciate its drying effect.

Warning: Patients who take MAOIs (see page 82) or who have glaucoma, enlarged prostate, or obstruction of the bladder should not take cyproheptadine. Cyproheptadine may negate the beneficial effects of the antidepressants.

Methysergide

Methysergide (Sansert) is one of the oldest preventive migraine medications and works both by blocking serotonin 2 receptors and by constricting blood vessels. Available as a 2 mg tablet, methysergide is usually taken three times a day.

At doses higher than 6 mg per day, side effects may be nausea, muscle cramps, and abdominal pain. Patients who use methysergide should stop taking it for 1 month after 6 months use to avoid its most serious side effect, retroperitoneal fibrosis (an overgrowth of the filmy connective tissue around certain organs deep in the abdomen). This usually disappears when methysergide is discontinued.

Warning: Patients with heart problems, such as coronary artery disease or peripheral vascular disease, history of inflammation in the leg veins, or stomach ulcers, or patients who may be pregnant should not take methysergide.

Methylergonovine

Methylergonovine (Methergine) is a related ergot that can be taken daily for prevention of migraine. It blocks serotonin 2 receptors and constricts blood vessels, as does methysergide. The starting dose for methylergonovine is a 0.2 mg tablet once per day; this is slowly increased to three times per day. The maximum dose is usually two tablets three times per day. Possible side effects include muscle aches (cramps in women), hallucinations (rarely), and signs of constricted blood vessels (such as chest pain).

Warning: Methylergonovine should not be used by anyone with heart disease, arterial disease, vein disease, high blood pressure, or possibility of pregnancy; it should not be taken continuously for more than 6 months without a "drug holiday."

NONSTEROIDAL ANTI-INFLAMMATORY DRUGS

The nonsteroidal anti-inflammatory drugs (NSAIDs) can be taken three times a day with food to help decrease the frequency of migraine (see Table 9-3). They may be highly effective, even when other drugs have not worked. Patients should be aware of stomach pain. These medications may work well for women whose migraines increase during the menstrual periods or ovulation because the drugs inhibit the production of prostaglandins, which cause inflammation and pain.

A new form of anti-inflammatories, the cyclooxygenase 2 (Cox-2) inhibitors, are being studied in the acute and preventive treatment of migraine. Unfortunately, they usually cause stomach problems such as ulcers as do the older NSAIDs. Three new Cox-2 inhibitor anti-inflammatory medications are celecoxib (Celebrex), rofecoxib (Vioxx), and valdecoxib (Bextra) (see page 68).

HORMONAL TREATMENT

Hormonal regulation and other techniques have been tried in women whose headaches occur mostly around their menstrual periods or when they ovulate. For a further discussion of headache and the menstrual cycle, refer to Chapter 16.

LEUKOTRIENE ANTAGONISTS

Leukotriene antagonists are antiasthma medications. The most commonly used are montelukast (Singulair) and zafirlukast (Accolate). A study performed at The New England Center for Headache suggests that these safe medications may also prevent migraine, especially in children.

ATYPICAL ANTIPSYCHOTIC MEDICATIONS

Don't let the word *psychotic* put you off. These medications intervene with another important chemical messenger involved in migraine, namely dopamine. There is anecdotal evidence that they are helpful in chronic migraine, unresponsive to the usual agents. These medications include quetiapine (Seroquel), olanzapine (Zyprexa), risperdal (Risperidone), and ziprasidone (Geodon). Each has advantages and disavantages depending on the clinical picture.

CHAPTER 11

TREATMENT OF CLUSTER HEADACHE WITH MEDICATION

Dr. David Dodick, a neurologist and headache specialist at the Mayo Clinic in Scottsdale, AZ, has divided treatment of cluster headache into four categories: acute, transitional, preventive, and surgical.

ACUTE TREATMENT

Oxygen

A cluster headache attack is best treated by breathing pure oxygen for up to 20 minutes at a rate of 7 L per hour through a loosely fitting mask that covers the mouth and nose. Relief can be dramatic! We recommend that patients sit on comfortable furniture, bending forward at the waist. This is often referred to as the *Rodin Thinker* position, after the famous sculpture. The cluster attack usually breaks in 20 minutes or less. The treatment can be repeated. In some cases, the oxygen lessens the pain, but the pain recurs when the oxygen is stopped. Oxygen works better when preventive treatment is being taken.

Triptans

A cluster headache can be stopped rapidly with a self-administered injection under the skin of sumatriptan (Imitrex) 6 mg, the only triptan formally studied and approved by the US Food and Drug Administration (FDA) as safe and effective. The injection generally works in under 15 minutes, and occasionally as quickly as 5 minutes, faster than oxygen.

Recently, sumatriptan nasal spray 20 mg has been found to be effective in stopping a cluster attack acutely. It works at the same rate as does oxygen. The maximum approved number of sumatriptan shots or sprays per day is two shots or two sprays, or one of each. Please see Chapter 9 for details about side effects.

One study demonstrated that zolmitriptan tablets 5 to 10 mg are effective in stopping cluster pain in 30 minutes or less, but this triptan has not yet been approved by the US FDA for this purpose. So far this is the only oral tablet that has been found to stop a cluster attack. The study proving its effectiveness was done in people whose cluster attacks lasted for at least 45 minutes.

Ergots
Ergotamine tartrate can be given by mouth (Cafergot), under the tongue, or as a rectal suppository (Cafergot) to stop an attack. An injection of dihydroergotamine (DHE 45) is often helpful. DHE 45 works rapidly intravenously.

Other Options
Daily use of opiates is not recommended, because of risk of dependency and rebound headache. A recent report cites the effectiveness of olanzapine (Zyprexa), an antipsychotic medication, in relieving nighttime attacks.

TRANSITIONAL TREATMENT

Treatment of cluster headache with a steroid is a means to relieve pain while establishing longer-acting preventive treatment. Steroids work rapidly to terminate cluster attacks, but they cannot be used long term because of possible side effects.

Prednisone is started at 60 mg per day and tapered gradually to nothing over a period of 10 days to 3 weeks. If, however, the cluster period has not ended when the steroid dose has decreased to a critically low level and traditional preventive medications have not been started, the cluster headaches usually return. Thus, the steroids and the preventive treatment should be started simultaneously. We have decreased the length of our steroid treatment from 3 weeks to 7 to 10 days to decrease the likelihood of the patient developing one of the serious side effects of long-term steroid use called *aseptic necrosis of bone.* This problem affects large joints such as the shoulder or hip and may necessitate a joint replacement. This is a very rare but serious side effect that can be decreased by shortening the treatment time.

Warning: Long-term use of prednisone (or any steroid) may cause the above or numerous other side effects and should be avoided.

PREVENTIVE TREATMENT

Verapamil, a calcium channel blocker, appears at present to be the most effective preventive treatment for cluster headache. The dosage is an 80 mg tablet taken three times per day; four to six such tablets (and rarely more) per day are occasionally required. Some patients are able to take the long-acting form of the pill twice per day, but we always start with the short-acting form. Please see Chapter 10 for details about the side effects.

Ergotamine tartrate, one tablet once or twice per day for several weeks, may prevent attacks from occurring; keep in mind that this treatment is not used in migraine as it increases the frequency of migraine attacks by causing a rebound syndrome. Also, if a patient takes ergotamine, he or she cannot take sumatriptan or zolmitriptan in the same 24 hours. Please see Chapter 9 for details about the side effects.

Lithium carbonate may also prevent cluster headache; 300 mg two or three times per day usually brings relief. Lithium can cause dry mouth and kidney and thyroid problems, and requires blood monitoring.

Divalproex sodium (Depakote) prevents cluster headache in some patients. We start our patients on 250 mg two or three times daily; then, if possible, we switch to them to Depakote ER 500 mg in a once-daily dose, increasing to 1,000 mg if necessary. See Chapter 10 for details about side effects.

Topiramate (Topamax) appears to be effective in preventing cluster. Doses higher than 75 to 150 mg are rarely necessary. Please see Chapter 10 for details of side effects.

Gabapentin (Neurontin) is another anticonvulsant that may be effective in preventing cluster at doses of 1,800 mg per day or higher. Please see Chapter 10 for details of side effects.

Methysergide (Sansert) 2 mg three times per day, or methylergonovine (Methergine) 0.2 mg three times per day, can be taken daily to prevent cluster headache for up to 6 months. On rare occasions the dosage must be doubled. Once again, if a person is taking methysergide or methylergonovine, he or she cannot take a triptan. Please refer to Chapter 10 for details of the side effects of methysergide and methylergonovine.

Other Options

One important feature of preventing cluster is that preventive medications for cluster often work better when combined. We refer to this treatment combination as *verapamil plus*. We begin our patients on verapamil and then add some combination of lithium and/or an antiepilepsy drug (anticonvulsant).

When no other medications have worked, indomethacin (Indocin), a nonsteroidal anti-inflammatory drug, is surprisingly helpful in some patients with cluster headache. Patients start at 25 mg three times per day with meals; indomethacin must be used with caution to reduce the risk of ulcer. We often add an acid-decreasing medication called a *proton pump inhibitor,* such as omeprazole (Prilosec), lansoprazole (Prevacid), pantoprazole (Protonix), or esomeprazole (Nexium), to protect the stomach from daily use of indomethacin.

Some patients respond to acetazolamide (Diamox), which is related to topiramate, starting at 250 mg three times per day.

Capsaicin, an extract of red peppers, has been investigated as a cluster headache preventive medicine by Dr. David Marks of The New England Center for Headache. Results suggest that it can help reduce pain after about 5 days of daily application inside the nostril on the side of the pain. It is available without prescription as Zostrix HP (0.075%) but should be used only under a doctor's direction. Civamide, a synthetic compound that is chemically related to capsaicin, may also be effective in preventing cluster. There are onging studies of a Civamide nasal spray given in both nostrils that appear promising.

Patients with severe cluster headache who do not respond to outpatient therapy should be admitted to a specialized inpatient headache unit for more aggressive care, which usually includes intravenous DHE 45. It almost always works. An older sometimes effective therapy is intravenous histamine desensitization. It has to be given cautiously as intravenous histamine can precipitate a severe cluster attack.

SURGICAL TREATMENT

Two surgical approaches to intractable cluster that does not respond to any therapy show promise. The first is called *radiofrequency trigeminal ablation (gangliorhizolysis)*. This involves destroying the branches of the trigeminal nerve that carry the pain of cluster. It is done while the patient is awake. A long needle is inserted in the cheek or mouth and advanced to an area just outside the brainstem. This treatment usually works, but it necessitates making the cornea of the eye on the treatment side permanently numb. This can lead to discomfort in that eye as a mild side effect.

The second approach, which is newer and more exciting, involves placing a radiostimulator deep into the brain at the site of the cluster generator in the hypothalamus. This has worked in six patients treated in Milano, Italy, by Drs. Massimo Leone and Gennaro Bussone, but has not yet been tried in other countries. There have been dramatic results from this procedure, without any complications.

Given the high rate of success with preventive medications, thankfully few people require consideration for surgery.

Chronic cluster headache is at times very difficult to treat; patients with this condition are the ones who occasionally need a surgical approach.

CONCLUSION

There are several effective treatments for the acute care and prevention of cluster headache. We often use them in combination. Only a few severe cases of chronic cluster need to be considered for surgical intervention.

CHAPTER 12

TREATMENT WITHOUT MEDICATION

At The New England Center for Headache, we share the belief of many clinicians that an appropriate combination of pharmacologic and nonpharmacologic (without medication) treatments can be more effective than either alone.

Nonpharmacologic treatment techniques can be classified as active and passive. Active techniques require patient involvement, responsibility, and participation, focusing on such activities as keeping headache calendars, making nutritional changes, exercising, practicing relaxation techniques, and modifying behavior that may contribute to headache. With passive techniques, patients simply receive treatments without modifying their behavior.

ACTIVE TECHNIQUES

The underlying concept that patients' behavior is key to the continuation or relief of any illness is the basis of behavioral medicine. Doctors and patients should review issues that might stand in the way of successful treatment. Because we recognize how difficult it can be to make changes in lifestyle, we provide our patients with clear instructions and initiate discussions about potential pitfalls. This chapter reviews important active techniques that may help you to deal with your headaches.

Headache Calendar

Headache calendars or diaries are daily logs of anything that might relate to your headaches and are vital to appropriate treatment. As we discuss how to use a headache calendar, refer to Figure 12-1A.

A headache calendar helps a patient record ongoing information about the frequency, intensity, and duration of headaches. It can also help patients monitor how and when

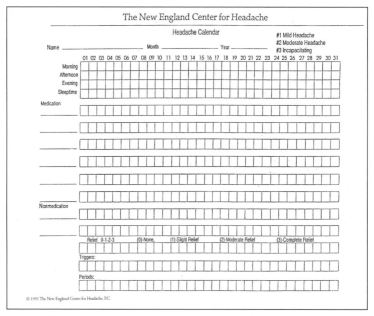

Figure 12-1A The front of the headache calendar used at our center.

to take medication, track its effectiveness, and document potential headache triggers. The calendar helps to show any relationship between headaches and a woman's menstrual cycle. Each calendar represents 1 month of headache activity. We ask our patients to record headache intensity, timing, medications used, and triggers. Both preventive and acute care medications must be listed. When listing acute care medications, patients record the degree of relief obtained, ranging from 0 for no relief to 3 for complete relief. Under the heading *Nonmedication*, patients record exercise, relaxation activities, and other recommended techniques. Figure 12-1B shows the reverse side of our calendar, which lists potential headache triggers. Patients record these elements under *Triggers* on the front of the calendar. To record the days of menstrual flow, women enter *X*s in the boxes labeled *Periods*. Finally, all medications—both prescription (from us and from

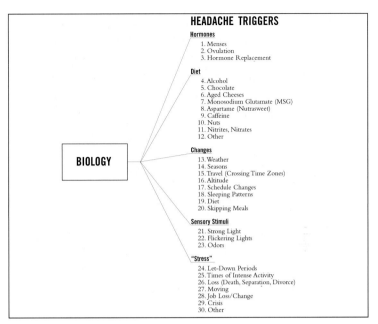

HEADACHE TRIGGERS

Hormones
1. Menses
2. Ovulation
3. Hormone Replacement

Diet
4. Alcohol
5. Chocolate
6. Aged Cheeses
7. Monosodium Glutamate (MSG)
8. Aspartame (Nutrasweet)
9. Caffeine
10. Nuts
11. Nitrites, Nitrates
12. Other

Changes
13. Weather
14. Seasons
15. Travel (Crossing Time Zones)
16. Altitude
17. Schedule Changes
18. Sleeping Patterns
19. Diet
20. Skipping Meals

Sensory Stimuli
21. Strong Light
22. Flickering Lights
23. Odors

"Stress"
24. Let-Down Periods
25. Times of Intense Activity
26. Loss (Death, Separation, Divorce)
27. Moving
28. Job Loss/Change
29. Crisis
30. Other

BIOLOGY

Figure 12-1B The back of the calendar.

other physicians) and off-the-shelf medications—must be recorded accurately.

These calendars help doctors to monitor their patients' progress. The first calendar is used as a baseline, and at follow-up visits the doctor reviews any changes in the calendar and records them as percent change from the baseline.

Patients who take frequent doses or large quantities of pain relievers or ergotamine use the calendars to follow a specific program, the goal of which is to decrease and eliminate daily use of these medications.

Relaxation Techniques

The goal of relaxation techniques is to reduce the intense "fight or flight" response and also the levels of substances the body produces in response to stress. Deep rhythmic breathing techniques are the basis of all relaxation strategies. To try deep rhythmic breathing, sit in a comfortable chair in a quiet environment; loosen your collar and belt, and close your eyes. Breathe in deeply and slowly, making sure that your abdomen moves more than your chest. At first, inhale to a count of 3, working your way up to 10 as you master the technique. When you reach your peak inhalation, hold it for a second or so and then let it out slowly to the same count. It may be helpful for you to focus on "inhaling relaxation" and "exhaling tension" as you do the exercise.

Progressive relaxation.   Tense your toes slowly as you inhale to a slow count and then relax them as you exhale. Then move up your body, alternately tensing and relaxing the muscles of your calves, thighs, buttocks, abdomen, back, fingers, arms, shoulders, neck, and—finally—the muscles of your head and jaw.

Autogenic training.   Try repeating a series of phrases to yourself to suggest changes such as feeling warmth and heaviness. You might, for example, repeat, "My legs are warm and heavy," while associating this with a pleasant feeling. Move up the body as described for progressive relaxation.

Visual imagery.   Help to relax the head and neck muscles by visualizing them as tight, scrunched, uneven, crooked, and crossing lines. Then focus on making the lines smoother, straighter, and evenly spaced. Visualize yourself on a sandy beach with your hands under the hot sand. Now feel the sand warm your hands (Figure 12-2).

Exercises that focus on warmth may help patients with migraine, many of whom tend to have cold hands and feet. Done successfully, visualization can divert blood flow from the head to the hands and/or feet while bringing on a state of relaxation.

Figure 12-2 Visual imagery—visualize yourself in a relaxing, beautiful place.

Body scan. Our colleagues Steven Baskin and Randall Weeks at The New England Institute for Behavioral Medicine in Stamford, CT, teach their patients how to perform a "body scan." They suggest that their patients remain alert for signs of tension in the head, neck, shoulders, arms, or legs throughout the day. Without realizing it, many people hunch their shoulders; this creates muscle tension in the shoulders, neck, and head. Or they may contract muscles around the neck or head, or clench their jaws or fists. People who check for these signs of tension throughout the day may be able to reduce muscle tension and decrease the effects of stress on the body. This type of body scan can be accompanied by deep breathing and other relaxation techniques.

Get in the habit of stopping what you are doing once every hour to check for signs of muscle tension and to take a quick deep-breathing/relaxation break. Relax with gentle neck rolls: allow your chin to fall to your chest, then gently rotate your head right and left 5 or 10 times (Figure 12-3). If

Figure 12-3 How to do a neck roll: flex your chin to your chest, then gently roll your head to either side 5 to 10 times.

you work at a computer for hours at a time, take a few minutes every hour or so to cup your hands over your eyes, giving your eyes a chance to rest.

Biofeedback. Biofeedback is commonly used in the treatment of both tension-type headache and migraine. It has not been found useful in cluster headache. Biofeedback may be administered by a clinical psychologist trained in the technique, or by a trained biofeedback technician. More effective in children but also helpful in adults, the goal is to reduce the symptoms and ultimately to eliminate the need for feedback.

Biofeedback is a "return of information" about biologic processes. It works because electronic equipment senses information such as temperature or muscle tension and gives you auditory or visual feedback over time. The combination of feedback and reinforcement helps you to control muscle tension, hand temperature, and other functions (Figure 12-4).

Cognitive Therapy
Cognition means *thinking*. Many people have negative feelings, and they translate these into such statements as, "I will

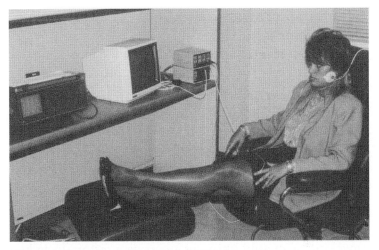
Figure 12-4A patient practicing biofeedback.

never get rid of my headaches." Cognitive therapists believe that if you can change your thoughts, you can change the feelings associated with these thoughts. Cognitive therapy has proven successful in treating anxiety disorders and depression. It has also proven useful in treating headache disorders. Psychologists and other health care professionals who practice cognitive therapy can help you challenge these negative thoughts, change your thinking, and ultimately change the way you feel. This can give you a more positive, optimistic, and less destructive way to think, feel, and be.

Psychotherapy
Psychotherapy alone has not been found useful as a headache treatment. If, however, headaches are accompanied by psychological difficulties, marital problems, job-related

difficulties, depression, anxiety, and other problems, psychotherapy can help.

Group therapy, particularly in the form of support groups, has been useful for headache sufferers as well as patients with a variety of chronic illnesses. Headache groups are currently being offered in cities throughout the United States by the American Council for Headache Education (ACHE) and the National Headache Foundation (NHF).

Lifestyle Changes

All of the techniques described in this chapter require you to review and modify various aspects of your lifestyle. Calendars can be useful in helping you to identify potential headache-provoking or stressful situations and trigger factors, including food. Remember to eat a healthful balanced diet at regular times each day. Exercise is vital for reducing headache and maintaining good health (Figure 12-5).

Since many patients focus on others' needs but leave little time for themselves, we suggest that our patients use an

Figure 12-5 Lifestyle changes—eat healthy foods and exercise regularly to feel good and reduce headaches.

appointment book to schedule time for themselves—"my time"—and to keep to the schedule (Figure 12-6).

PASSIVE TECHNIQUES

Acupuncture

Acupuncture, an ancient Asian healing art, involves placing needles in the skin at specific points. Acupuncture corrects what are termed *imbalances* between the two parts (*yin* and *yang*) of a life force known as *ch'i*. Applied correctly, the needles cause minimal or no pain or discomfort. If you have no response after six to eight sessions, acupuncture probably will not work for you. Most patients say that acupuncture eliminates any pain they are having at the time, but that it is not able to prevent pain in the future.

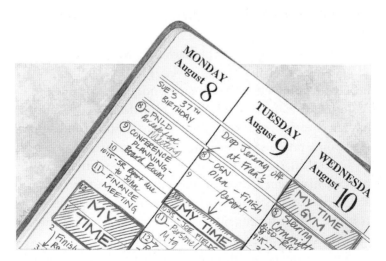

Figure 12-6 Use an appointment book or personal digital assistant to schedule "my time" regularly.

Acupressure

Acupressure is a technique based on acupuncture. Some have found using the thumb and forefinger to squeeze the web between the thumb and forefinger of the other hand effective in aborting migraine. For tension-type headache, pressure can be applied to the small indentations approximately midway between the outer border of the eye and the inner border of the ear and also at the back of the head.

Chiropractic Therapy

Chiropractic therapy is based on the theory that most diseases of the body are a result of misalignment of the vertebral column. The goal of the treatment is to realign the vertebrae through the use of manual techniques called *adjustment*. Many neurologists question the validity of chiropractic therapy and are concerned that aggressive manipulation, or adjustments, of the neck may injure important structures such as the blood vessels that supply the brain.

Physical and Occupational Therapies

Physical therapy has been used in headache disorders and, in particular, in tension-type headache, in which the neck and shoulder muscles may be involved. Heat and massage have been used as muscle relaxants since antiquity, and newer techniques, such as ultrasound, that deliver deep heat to muscles have been shown to be helpful in reducing spasm and tenderness. Some patients get relief by taking a warm shower.

Electrical stimulation may also be beneficial. Many patients may benefit from improvement in posture and gait, and these patients may be given appropriate exercises to do at home. Other treatments such as active and passive stretching increase the range of motion about the neck.

Some patients' occupations contribute to muscle tension. Administrative personnel, telephone representatives, and those who use computers may all develop tense muscles in their backs and necks as well as postural problems that contribute to tension-type headache. Frequent breaks and professional attention to posture may help.

Application of cold to the head may help to constrict dilated blood vessels, override pain transmission, numb the skin, and reduce metabolic activity in muscles, contributing to the relief of pain. Studies have shown, and many of our patients agree, that the "headache ice-pillow" is useful. The molded pillow fits comfortably at the back of the head and neck, and holds a frozen gel pack that ices the neck. Ice applied to the forehead, eyes, and temples can also be helpful.

Massage Therapy
Massage can reduce muscle tension in various parts of the body, and it can reduce headache. A variety of techniques are practiced by licensed massage therapists.

Trigger Point Injections
Located in various parts of the body, trigger points are small areas that feel like knots of muscle tissue; they are tender to touch and may refer pain to various areas of the head. The exact cause of trigger points is not fully understood. However, an injection of local anesthetic into these tender points can be helpful.

Transcutaneous Electrical Nerve Stimulation
Transcutaneous electrical nerve stimulation (TENS) blocks the transmission of pain with electrodes placed on the skin between the pain and the brain. This therapy has proven successful in treating other types of chronic pain, but at this time the results of TENS therapy for headache have been somewhat disappointing. A new type of low-intensity stimulation to the ear lobe has been tested but is not widely used. Magnets also have been tried, sometimes with beneficial results.

NATUROPATHY AND HOMEOPATHY

Naturopathy and homeopathy represent alternatives to traditional medical treatments and are attractive to some patients who want to avoid pharmacologic therapy. Naturopathy uses only natural physical forces such as air, sunshine, water, and heat. Homeopathy uses natural substances as well as minute amounts of the active ingredients in some medications. Traditional physicians would consider the amounts of these medications used to be far too small to produce a therapeutic response and attribute any effects to a placebo response. All the same, some patients state that they have benefited from these approaches.

HERBAL, MINERAL, AND VITAMIN THERAPIES

Do not use any of the following substances without *first checking with your doctor.*

Feverfew

A variety of herbal therapies has been used to prevent migraine, the most popular of which has been feverfew, which is derived from the chrysanthemum family of plants. A recent large review of all of the studies on this herb was inconclusive as to its benefits. Feverfew is available in several forms and dosages and is usually found in health food stores.

Magnesium

Magnesium is a trace element found in the body. Some scientific evidence suggests that magnesium levels are lower in the brains of migraine patients. Use of magnesium to treat migraine is under study. We recommend using 400 to 600 mg per day of chelated magnesium as long as it does not produce diarrhea. The evidence for the effectiveness of magnesium in headache prevention seems to be strongest for menstrually associated migraine and migraine with aura.

Vitamin Therapies

Dr. Jean Schoenen, a professor of neurology in Liege, Belgium, has reported that vitamin B_2 (riboflavin) fares significantly better than does placebo in preventing headache when taken in a dose of 400 mg per day for 3 to 4 months. He also believes that riboflavin is more likely to be helpful in people who have migraine with aura.

Recently Professor Silberstein and colleagues at the Jefferson Headache Clinic in Philadelphia, PA, published a trial of 150 mg of coenzyme Q_{10} each day in recurrent migraine with promising results.

We suggest 400 international units of vitamin E daily. High doses of vitamin A are not only potentially toxic, they may cause headache. Doses of 150 mg or greater of vitamin B_6 can cause harm to peripheral nerves, so we have stopped recommending this therapy. Some claim vitamin C helps headache; however, results are inconsistent.

Garlic and Ginger

Ginger clearly reduces nausea for some people and can be taken during pregnancy and for frequent nauseating migraines. Some patients have found that garlic has properties that might be useful in migraine.

Ginseng

Ginseng is said to decrease tension and relieve headache. It is available as a tea and in capsules, tablets, and dried root powder. *Ginkgo biloba* and valerian root have been touted as effective by patients.

Guarana

In Brazil guarana is a popular headache remedy (it is even contained in pop drinks). Guarana contains caffeine.

CONCLUSION

A number of treatments alternative to pharmacologic therapy are available. Some of these techniques may be helpful to
you, and others may not. Keep in mind, however, that an
immediate and permanent cure for migraine has not yet
been discovered.

CHAPTER 13

PATIENT-DOCTOR RELATIONSHIP

We feel that an educated patient is a patient who has the potential to experience optimal headache relief. You should know as much as possible about your headaches, your treatment plan, and the medications you take. Sometimes the amount and type of information a patient receives are defined by the doctor-patient relationship.

Roter and Hall, in their book *Doctors Talking with Patients/Patients Talking with Doctors**, describe a number of different types of doctor-patient relationships. We feel that the mutual doctor-patient relationship yields the most positive treatment outcome. Thus, we urge you to find a physician who is open to this style and who will take the time to listen to you, hear your concerns, educate you, and give you feedback about your condition, treatment options, and medications (Figure 13-1).

Your doctor should accept the validity, reality, intensity, and quality of your pain. He or she should do the following:
- Accept your complaints, not dismiss them as unimportant
- Take the time to listen to you
- Understand headache. It is all right to ask if he or she sees many headache patients and what the success rate is.
- Seem compassionate and understanding
- Seem flexible about exploring a variety of treatment options
- Take the time to discuss findings, diagnosis, and treatment plan as well as alternative treatments
- Answer your questions to your satisfaction
- Tell you what to expect from treatment (prognosis)
- Tell you what medication is being prescribed, how it works, how frequently to take it and when, and what side

---

*Roter DL, Hall JA. Doctors talking with patients/patients talking with doctors. Westport (CT): Auburn Health; 1992.

Figure 13-1 A good doctor-patient relationship is based on trust and leads to more effective therapy.

effects it may cause. Your doctor should note significant drug interactions (including alcohol) and tell you which off-the-shelf medications to avoid. He or she should say how long you will need to take the medication, how and when to reduce or increase the dosage, and how or when to discontinue it.

- Describe to you any tests ordered and their purposes, and explain how the results will be used
- Discuss with you nonpharmacologic interventions related to changes in your lifestyle (sleep habits, diet, exercise, and work conditions). In addition, your doctor should express interest in how you plan to make these changes.

It is a good idea to write down all your questions before a visit to any doctor. These questions should include how to contact the doctor when the office is closed, and who the contact is when your doctor is not on call. Be sure to ask whether your doctor has a specific "telephone time" for taking calls; many do.

Remember, taking a cooperative active role in the treatment of your headache improves your chances of success. Good doctor-patient communication is an important beginning.

CHAPTER 14

EMERGENCY DEPARTMENT AND HOSPITAL TREATMENT

Your treatment plan should include several levels of intervention for home care to decrease the likelihood of your needing emergency care. Back-up or rescue medication may be needed for occasional headache attacks.

If you have to go to an emergency room, go with someone who can take you home; the staff might otherwise be reluctant to give you strong pain or antinausea medications, which might sedate you. Although some emergency rooms are set up for headache patients, most put patients with headache in noisier colder brighter rooms than are ideal. You may have a long wait as the staff will not consider you as sick as some of the more critically ill patients. With this in mind, we suggest that you take with you a sweatshirt, dark glasses, and patience (Figure 14-1). Since emergency room staff may suspect headache patients of drug-seeking behavior, we

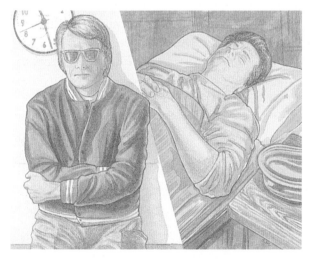

Figure 14-1 Headache patients in emergency rooms. If you must go, bring a sweatshirt, dark glasses, and patience.

provide our patients with cards that identify them as migraine sufferers, suggest appropriate treatment to the emergency room nurse and physician, and list our phone number if the staff wants to verify information with us.

In a "headache-friendly emergency room," you can expect to be ushered into a dimly lit quiet room where you receive a blanket to keep you warm and a basin in case you vomit (see Figure 14-1). The staff will evaluate you appropriately, and if you say you are having pain typical of one of your migraine attacks, you will probably be treated quickly with little testing. If, however, you raise any of the red flags (see Chapter 5), you may undergo further evaluation. This can be very helpful if there is something new going on, but it can be repetitive, costly, and time consuming if you are experiencing a typical severe migraine.

MIGRAINE TREATMENT

If you have intermittent migraine and need acute care, you may be lucky enough to receive injectable dihydroergotamine (DHE 45), sumatriptan (Imitrex), or intravenous treatments including steroids, ketorolac (an anti-inflammatory medication), and/or valproate (Depacon), which are the best injectable medications currently available to stop a migraine attack. Antinausea medications may be administered, and these are excellent as well. Far less helpful are the opiates. Injections of meperidne (pethidine) hydrochloride (Demerol) and promethazine hydrochloride (Phenergan) or other antinausea medications are the most common cocktail used in US emergency rooms.

DHE 45
DHE 45 (see Chapter 9) has been available for half a century and can be injected intramuscularly, intravenously, or under the skin (subcutaneously). Given alone, DHE 45 gets rid of

headache for a long time and often reduces nausea. When our patients go to the emergency room, we recommend that they receive three injections: DHE 45; dexamethasone (Decadron), a steroid; and promethazine (Phenergan) for nausea. The anti-inflammatory ketorolac (Toradol) can be substituted for the steroid or the DHE 45.

Sumatriptan

Sumatriptan (Imitrex) is a 6 mg injection given under the skin (see Chapter 9); it can be self-injected at home to avoid the emergency room visit, but it is sometimes given in the emergency room as well. More than 80% of people treated with sumatriptan report significant relief and are usually free of headache after 1 hour. If less than 100 mg of sumatriptan has been taken earlier at home, an injection can be given. If any other triptan has been taken earlier that day, sumatriptan cannot be given.

Miscellaneous Medications

Antinausea medications. Prochlorperazine (Compazine) 5 to 10 mg can be given intravenously over 10 minutes and may help knock out a headache. Sometimes it causes tightening of the muscles as a side effect, which usually responds to a small intravenous dose of diphenhydramine (Benadryl). Metoclopramide (Reglan) 10 mg given intravenously can block nausea as well as headache, often without sedation. It can also cause tightening of muscles and occasionally some irritability. Other related medications given intravenously include promethazine (Phenergan) and droperidol (Anapsine). Recently droperidol has been associated with liver dysfunction. Chlorpromazine (Thorazine), which is in the same group of medications, can be given either intravenously or by rectal suppository and tends to make patients sleepy and/or lower their blood pressure. When given intravenously, it is often preceded by intravenous fluids to prevent the lowering of blood pressure. Finally, ondansetron (Zofran) and granisetron (Kytril) given intravenously stop nausea rapidly and do not cause drowsiness or other side effects. (See Chapter 9 for more details.)

Valproate. Intravenous valproate sodium (Depacon), an antiepilepsy medication, and the injectable form of divalproex sodium (Depakote), used for epilepsy, migraine, and psychiatric problems (see Chapter 10), appear to be useful in stopping migraine pain rapidly. They appear to have fewer side effects when given intravenously than when taken orally.

Opiates. Rarely do we prescribe opiates (narcotics), both because they usually do not work well to stop migraine and because they can cause dependency. These powerful painkillers can be tried if all else fails, if the patient has already taken a triptan or an ergot, or the patient has vascular disease and cannot take medication that affects blood vessels (see Chapter 9). Injectable opiates such as meperidine (Demerol) or morphine should be used no more than once per month, and tablet forms no more than one day per week. Some emergency rooms have taken meperidine out of the pharmacy as it can cause many side effects including making people irritable or drowsy, and the beneficial effect often does not last very long.

An opiate is often given with an antinausea agent such as promethazine (Phenergan) or a combined antinausea agent/antihistamine, hydroxyzine (Vistaril). Butorphanol (Stadol) can be given by injection or nasal spray. It rapidly relieves pain, may cause drowsiness or dizziness, and does not usually produce euphoria (a "high"). It is probably the most habit forming of all of the narcotics. It can be helpful when used occasionally in small doses. When not used properly, it causes side effects and dependency.

Conclusion

At-home medication is better than ER medication. If you can avoid going to the emergency room for treatment by having powerful enough medication for home treatment, you will be better off. This almost always means using a triptan, sometimes with a rescue or back-up medication.

CLUSTER HEADACHE TREATMENT

If you must go to the emergency room during an attack of cluster headache, chances are the attack will be breaking by the time you get treatment. Oxygen inhalation is the most effective and safest treatment. Patients who receive oxygen should be seated, bending slightly forward; the oxygen mask should fit loosely over the nose and mouth and should deliver 7 to 10 L per minute.

Ergotamine tartrate by mouth or under the tongue can be helpful, but DHE 45 by injection works faster. Sumatriptan (Imitrex) injection usually aborts a cluster attack within 5 to 10 minutes.

Pain medication is not specific for cluster headache, but it may decrease the intensity of the pain if nothing else has worked. Cluster patients must not use opiates (narcotics) on a daily basis as they will become dependent on them, especially if they have chronic cluster that does not go into remission (a dormant phase).

See Chapter 11 for a detailed discussion of cluster headache treatment.

SPECIALIZED INPATIENT THERAPY

When headaches occur daily, are severe and incapacitating, and when they are associated with disability, decreased quality of life, or rebound syndromes from analgesic and/or ergotamine or triptan overuse, aggressive therapy with intravenous medication and cautious withdrawal of the offending medications must begin.

Although treatment can be attempted on an outpatient basis, many patients with severe withdrawal symptoms must be hospitalized, and a well-staffed properly designed interdisciplinary hospital program directed by headache specialists may yield marked improvement and long-lasting benefits.

Patients who take butalbital-containing medications, ergots, tranquilizers, or opiates everyday are usually best detoxified in a hospital setting to ensure that serious withdrawal symptoms such as epileptic seizures, tremors, insomnia, anxiety, diarrhea, and incapacitating rebound pain do not occur; if they do occur, appropriate medical support is available.

CONCLUSION

Several levels of migraine treatment should be provided to patients in an attempt to avoid trips to the emergency department. Although we agree that it is preferable to treat patients appropriately on an outpatient basis, our experience has shown us that this is not always possible. Thus, we are convinced that under certain circumstances inpatient headache treatment is appropriate and necessary, and ultimately cost effective.

CHAPTER 15

HEADACHE IN CHILDREN

Children are not immune to headache; the youngest patient to visit our center was only 3 years old when she first came to see us. Her mother reported that the child seemed to experience severe headaches since the age of 6 months. Three or four times per year the little girl would become distraught, vomit, and cry inconsolably. The mother related that the child pressed the same side of her head to her mother's chest each time she had an attack (Figure 15-1). All medical examinations and tests were completely within normal limits. Between episodes, the child was happy and content.

Figure 15-1 A small child with an occasional severe headache presses her head to her mother's chest.

When the child was old enough to describe her pain, it became clear that she was experiencing headache.

Headaches are less common in children than in adults. Studies show that 39% of 6-year-olds get occasional headaches, as do 70% of 15-year-olds and 90% of adults. Approximately the same number of boys get headaches as do girls. Migraine occurs slightly more often in 8- to 11-year-old boys than in girls of the same age range. From puberty on, migraine occurs three times more often in girls and women than in boys and men.

DESCRIPTION OF HEADACHE TYPES

The majority of headaches in children are migraine and/or tension-type headaches, rather than headaches due to a serious underlying medical problem. Migraine in children tends to occur more frequently on both sides of the head than on one side, and attacks are usually shorter than are those in adults, lasting sometimes only for 1 to 2 hours. The headaches may not throb, but, rather, are steady and squeezing or pressure-type headaches. Children's attacks can come on rapidly and become intense in a short period of time. A child suffering from headache almost always appears pale and ill, and may complain of nausea and then vomit. A child may also exhibit a strong urge to sleep. Although sleep brings migraine relief throughout life, it seems to be especially effective for children, who can awaken after 1 or 2 hours and go out to play feeling absolutely fine.

Children often describe tension-type headache as a mild headache on both sides of the head or as a steady, nonthrobbing, squeezing, pressing, or aching in the forehead or at the top of the head. Headaches such as these should not cause concern; they usually respond to relaxation techniques, biofeedback training, altered diet, or small amounts of off-the-shelf medication. We recommend, however, that children under the age of 15 years avoid using ASA because it has been associated with Reye's syndrome. Of off-the-shelf medication, we recommend anti-inflammatory medicines such as ibuprofen (Advil or Motrin), naproxen sodium (Aleve), or ketoprofen (Orudis KT). Acetaminophen (such as in Tylenol) can also be helpful. Of prescription medicine, we prefer Midrin, which contains a mild blood vessel constrictor called isometheptene. We prefer not to use butalbital-containing medication such as Fiorinal or any of the opiates.

Children may develop daily chronic tension-type headache that can be very difficult to treat. The overuse of pain medication can lead to analgesic rebound headaches in patients, worsening the problem and making it harder to treat.

WHEN TO WORRY

Although most headaches in children are not serious, parents should watch for the following danger symptoms and signs that should prompt them to seek medical attention promptly:

- Headache with fever. This may be due to an infection, which could involve the brain or sinuses.
- Stiff neck and vomiting, with or without fever. This may be caused by meningitis (an inflammation of the covering of the brain and spinal cord) and requires immediate medical attention.
- Fever, confusion, and drowsiness. Immediate medical attention is needed to rule out a viral infection of the brain (encephalitis). It is uncommon, but it does occur.
- Fever, bull's-eye rash, history of a tick bite, joint pains, back pain, and weakness on one side of the face or in one arm or leg. These symptoms can indicate Lyme disease and should be evaluated immediately because Lyme disease can be cured if treated early.
- Slowly progressive headache. If a child has headache that steadily worsens over a period of days or weeks, especially

if the headache is present early in the morning and is associated with drowsiness, visual complaints, weakness, numbness, incoordination or speech problems, nausea, or vomiting, the child should be evaluated immediately. Although it is unlikely for a child to develop a brain tumor or blood clot, it must be ruled out if these symptoms are present.

- Headaches brought on by exertion. Some children complain that they get headaches when they participate in physical exercise. This is usually a benign (not serious) exertional headache or migraine triggered by exercise. Only rarely is this caused by a neurologic problem, but it should be evaluated.
- After head trauma (injury), most children develop brief headaches that disappear within 1 to 2 days. If the headaches are intense and associated with nausea, vomiting, drowsiness, or any other neurologic symptoms, the child should be seen by a doctor immediately.

EVALUATION

Although medical conditions may play a role in childhood headache, they do not commonly cause recurrent headaches. Refer to Chapter 6 for information about appropriate examinations and testing. Children should be told what to expect from diagnostic tests; this helps to reduce anxiety and encourages them to cooperate.

"MIGRAINE EQUIVALENTS"

Unexplained symptoms that some consider migraine related may be more common in children than in adults. Some children experience unexplained episodes of abdominal pain associated with nausea and vomiting, but no headache. Some doctors believe that these episodes may be caused by the same brain mechanisms that cause migraine, and term these pains *abdominal migraine*. Other migraine equivalents may include cyclical vomiting, in which children vomit profusely from time to time, but for which no cause can be found.

Finally, we note that our adult migraine patients are much more likely to have had motion sickness and car sickness as children than people who do not suffer from migraine.

PSYCHOLOGICAL FACTORS

Although psychological factors are not a major cause of headache in most children, they do contribute in some cases. If headaches are chronic, or do not respond to the usual treatments, it is appropriate to evaluate the role of stress and social and psychological factors. Children often express their reaction to family conflict through physical complaints. If they are already prone to migraine, they may complain of an increased frequency of headaches.

A small percentage of adolescents experience chronic daily headache. Some studies have shown that adolescents with chronic daily headache who do not respond well to treatment show evidence of depression, which must be treated. A few children have chronic daily headache that responds neither to headache therapy nor to psychotherapy. Although this pattern is not yet well understood and is difficult to treat, most "outgrow" their chronic headache by the time they complete high school or college.

Anxiety may play a role in some children's headaches, and our goal is to make the children's lives as normal as possible. The majority of these children become disabled and must be tutored at home when their condition becomes severe. Therefore, we ask school officials for flexible programming and to make arrangements for a rest area for timeout as needed, along with any other measures to keep them in school for as many hours as possible. Some school systems are much more cooperative than others, and the patients reap the benefits.

Families and doctors should cooperate with school officials to help them realize that these children suffer from a neurobiologically based disorder and need understanding and psychological and medical help if they are to overcome it.

TREATMENT

Pharmacologic Treatment

With some exceptions, the medications used to treat headaches in children are similar to those given to adults. We tend to use an absolute minimum amount of medication— just enough, no more—and rely as much as possible on non-pharmacologic interventions. As with adults, pharmacologic treatments fall into three categories: symptomatic, specific (acute care), and preventive.

Symptomatic therapy.   These measures address the pain and nausea and may include off-the-shelf medication, in appropriate dosages and frequency. Children, too, can develop rebound headache and should not take medication on a daily basis for extended periods.

Due to the risk of Reye's syndrome, we recommend that acetaminophen (Tylenol), ibuprofen (Advil, Nuprin, Motrin), naproxen sodium (Aleve), or ketoprofen (Orudis KT) be used instead of ASA. For more severe headaches, Tylenol with codeine may be used safely on an occasional basis. Antinausea medication should be used as appropriate in small doses. We favor promethazine (Phenergan) 12.5 or 25 mg by mouth for those who are not vomiting and by suppository for those who are vomiting. Emetrol is an effective off-the-shelf liquid antinausea medicine with no side effects.

Specific acute care agents. When prescription medications are needed for children over the age of 6 years, our first recommendation is for a combination of isometheptene, dichloralphenazone, and acetaminophen (Midrin), which can be given with or without antinausea medication. Children tolerate this combination well, and the capsule contents can be mixed into a tablespoon of apple sauce for those who cannot swallow capsules. The dose is one capsule at the start of a headache; this may be repeated in 1 hour if the headache persists. When stronger medications are needed, we sometimes prescribe butalbital, acetaminophen, and caffeine (Fioricet or Esgic), or the same without caffeine (Phrenilin). The dose is one tablet at the start of a headache. We prefer to work in cooperation with pediatricians and family doctors to determine what might be best for a given child.

When prescription nonsteroidal anti-inflammatory agents are appropriate, we often prescribe rofecoxib (Vioxx), naproxen sodium (Anaprox, available off-the-shelf as Aleve), or meclofenamate (Meclomen). In more severe cases and on rare occasions in children who are 10 years or older, we sometimes prescribe small doses of ergotamine if we do not want to use a triptan.

When migraine is persistent and unresponsive to treatment, some headache specialists give small doses of dihydroergotamine (DHE 45) intravenously or by injection to break the cycle. Sumatriptan (Imitrex) 20 mg nasal spray has been found to be safe and effective in adolescent migraine, and has been submitted to the US Food and Drug Administration (FDA) for review for official approval for use. Although not yet approved by the FDA for use by those under the age of 18 years, all the available triptans are prescribed in small doses for children on a regular basis by pediatric neurologists and headache specialists.

Preventive medication. When children have frequent, severe headaches that interfere with their lives, one of our first lines of defense is cyproheptadine (Periactin), an antihistamine available in both liquid and tablet forms, given at bedtime. The dosage is 2 to 12 mg daily. The majority of children respond well to this regimen, which we decrease or discontinue after 3 to 6 months of successful treatment. We generally reserve use of the tricyclic antidepressants (nortriptyline [Pamelor], amitriptyline [Elavil], or imipramine [Tofranil]) for adolescents, and we prescribe them only in small doses. β-Blockers such as propranolol (Inderal), nadolol (Corgard), and atenolol (Tenormin) may be effective, as may antiseizure medications such as gabapentin (Neurontin). We sometimes prescribe divalproex sodium (Depakote, Epival) for adolescents but not for younger children to avoid liver problems. The new Depakote ER form can be given just once in 24 hours and may have fewer side effects.

Most children with migraine have fewer attacks during the summer, perhaps because their schedules are more flexible without the pressures of school, and their preventive medication can be discontinued.

Nonpharmacologic Interventions

We try as much as possible to treat headache, especially in children, with nondrug alternatives. Chapter 12, "Treatment without Medication," reviews many of these techniques.

In children as in adults, we evaluate the role of diet, daily exercise, appropriate rest, and regulation of the sleep-wake cycle; we also look for potential trigger factors. Children who are old enough should maintain their own headache calendars to record their headache frequency and intensities, medication use, and triggers. We try to avoid having the calendars viewed as more "homework," and encourage parents to let their children keep their own calendars. Parents should not focus on one type of trigger or another because undue emphasis, for example, on dietary triggers may cue some children to become "dietary cripples."

Children respond very well to biofeedback and seem to enjoy working with the biofeedback computers and caregivers. When we notice clear-cut psychological issues or unhealthy family situations, we refer patients and their families for appropriate therapy, but we continue to focus our efforts on the biologic aspects of headache disorders. Children's headaches are not imagined any more than are adults' headaches.

CONCLUSION

Many children experience headache, and most of these headaches are not signs of serious disease. In most cases a combination of pharmacologic and nonpharmacologic treatments helps to relieve headache while enhancing children's quality of life.

CHAPTER 16

HORMONES AND HEADACHE IN WOMEN

Migraine is three times more common in women than in men, which is why we have devoted a chapter specifically to women and migraine. Prior to puberty, migraine occurs slightly more frequently in boys than in girls, but after menarche (a girl's first period), its prevalence among women increases dramatically, suggesting that it may be related to fluctuating female hormones, specifically estrogen.

Women's susceptibility to migraine increases at the stages in life outlined in Table 16-1.

The menstrual cycle represents a finely tuned balance between hormones produced by the brain's pituitary gland and the hypothalamus and those released by the ovaries. The uterus itself produces hormones called *prostaglandins* that can cause premenstrual cramps, painful menstruation, and headache. Marked by a rise in estrogen and progesterone levels, ovulation (when eggs are released from the ovaries) occurs at midcycle, usually between the eleventh and fourteenth days of the cycle. Hormone levels begin to rise after midcycle and then fall before menses, as shown in Figure 16-1. When progesterone levels fall, the lining of the uterus sheds and

Table 16-1 Times at which Women's Susceptibility to Migraine Increases
Menarche (onset of periods)
Start of each menstrual cycle
Use of oral contraceptives
Early pregnancy
Postpartum period
Perimenopause (time entering menopause)
Postmenopause (time after menopause)
Use of hormone replacement therapy such as estrogen and progesterone

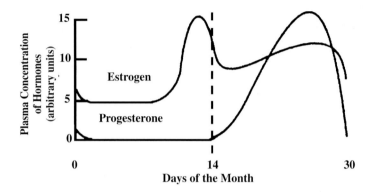

Figure 16-1 The monthly female hormonal cycle (variations of hormone levels during the month).

bleeding—menses—occurs. The first day of bleeding is considered day 1 of the cycle.

MENARCHE

Girls become more susceptible to migraine after they have their first menstrual period; one-third of all women with migraine experience their first attack within the year after their first period. It appears that the normal cycle of hormones, especially falling estrogen levels, affects brain, nerve, and blood vessel mechanisms involved in producing migraine.

MENSTRUAL MIGRAINE

According to some experts, *menstrual migraine* is defined as that occurring only between 2 days before a period and 3 days after it starts. Headaches that occur then and also at other times are often called *menstrually associated migraine*. Others define menstrual migraine more loosely as any headache that occurs at predictable times during the menstrual cycle. Sixty percent of women with migraine have more headaches just before or during their periods. These headaches can be the longest lasting and worst attacks of the month and can be the most difficult to treat. Some women report an increase in headache at midcycle when they ovulate (day 13 or 14).

Occasionally in the past, some of our patients have successfully used estradiol-17β (Estrace)—a synthetic estrogen—which is placed under the tongue (sublingually) when a migraine occurs during a period. The estradiol may stop the attack, reduce its intensity, or make it more responsive to the usual medications. However, the strategy does not always work, and triptans stop menstrual migraines more reliably and rapidly and have, for the most part, replaced this treatment.

Menstrual Migraine Treatment

Treatment of menstrual migraine involves previously discussed pharmacologic and nonpharmacologic interventions. These headaches differ from other migraines only in their timing in relation to the menstrual cycle and in that they are triggered by falling estrogen levels just before menstruation. They may last longer than migraines at other times in the cycle, although this speculation is controversial.

For women whose headaches occur mostly around the time of menses, we prescribe daily preventive medications, but only for those days leading up to, or during, the projected headache period, rather than throughout the entire month. This approach is called *pulsed therapy* or *miniprevention*. Refer to Chapter 10 for a description of preventive medications. We recommend that patients start preventive medication 2 to 3 days before the expected menstrual headache or 5 days before the expected period and continue the medication until menstrual flow stops. The nonsteroidal anti-inflammatory drugs, such as naproxen sodium (Anaprox or Aleve), meclofenamate (Meclomen), flurbiprofen (Ansaid), ketoprofen (Orudis), and ibuprofen (Motrin, Nuprin, Advil, and Medipren), have proven especially useful and should be taken two to three times per day with meals. Some patients respond well to once-a-day dosing with the new cyclooxygenase 2 inhibitor anti-inflammatory drugs rofecoxib (Vioxx), 25 or 50 mg, celecoxib (Celebrex), 200 mg, or valdecoxib (Bextra), 10 to 20 mg. They are long acting and cause fewer gastrointestinal side effects.

Sometimes we prescribe other preventive medications such as the antihistamine cyproheptadine (Periactin), β-blockers, antidepressants, calcium channel blockers, methyl-ergonovine (Methergine), and methysergide (Sansert). Daily use of bromocriptine (Parlodel) has been prescribed to increase brain levels of the chemical dopamine, but we have found it hard to use and not very beneficial.

Dr. Lawrence Newman, director of the St. Lukes-Roosevelt Headache Clinic and clinical associate professor of neurology at the Albert Einstein College of Medicine in New York, studied the use of sumatriptan (Imitrex). He found that sumatriptan 25 mg taken three times a day beginning 2 days before the expected onset of menstrual migraine and maintained for 5 days was effective in preventing the attacks. He and colleagues then published a large scientific study that showed that naratriptan (Amerge) 1 mg twice daily used in the same way also prevented or significantly reduced the frequency of the menstrual migraines.

Hormonal manipulation may be helpful as migraine is often induced by falling estrogen levels prior to menses. Boosting estrogen levels with small doses starting 5 days before menses may prevent or decrease the severity of attacks. We prefer the use of an estrogen skin patch to the tablets. Small doses of estrogen given for this purpose generally do not affect the periods. Other stronger agents can totally suppress menses and help headache, but this more powerful treatment is usually reserved for women who are significantly disabled for a week each month from migraine associated with menses.

Progesterone should probably not be given for headache control as it can worsen headache. When given along with estrogen to postmenopausal women, instead of being prescribed in high doses (10 mg) for 10 days, it should be started in low doses (2.5 mg) daily. Injections of long-acting progesterone (Depo-Provera) should be avoided as they may increase headache, and will do so for a full 3 months until the progesterone wears off. It is a good idea to have the doctor who treats your headaches consult with your gynecologist if hormonal strategies are contemplated.

Migraine attacks should be treated with standard therapies to abort migraine or lessen the pain (as described in Chapter 9). The focus should be on the triptans, which work faster and more completely than the ergots, but ergotamine with caffeine (Cafergot) or dihydroergotamine (DHE 45, Migranal) can be tried if the triptans fail.

Migraine attacks in women who take oral contraceptives ("the pill") generally occur during estrogen withdrawal, just prior to or at the start of menses. Sometimes the pill needs to be stopped if headache becomes more severe or frequent or is associated with neurologic symptoms such as weakness or numbness on one side. There is no evidence in the literature that hysterectomy is a reasonable treatment for menstrual migraine. In fact, it often worsens headache.

ORAL CONTRACEPTIVE USE

The effect of oral contraceptives on migraine is controversial. We believe that if migraine increases in frequency or becomes more severe when a woman takes oral contraceptives, then it is wise to discontinue their use. If the migraine is stable in a patient who already takes oral contraceptives, we do not suggest that they be discontinued. Patients who experience migraine with aura have a slightly increased chance of having a stroke than do women without migraine. Women who have migraine with long visual auras (greater than an hour in length), or auras with weakness, double vision, fainting, and vertigo (hemiplegic and basilar migraines) should not take oral contraceptives due to a possible greater increase in the risk of stroke. Smoking, of course, is associated with a much more significant risk of stroke than are oral contraceptives. Smokers face a risk of stroke 10 times that associated with migraine and oral contraceptives. So, if you smoke and have migraine, particularly migraine with aura, ask your doctor about the use of the pill, and stop smoking now!

When oral contraceptives are implicated in migraine, women who discontinue them may not notice improvement for 6 to 12 months. Each woman must decide for herself whether a potential improvement in migraine is counterbalanced by the risk of pregnancy or a return of gynecologic symptoms that oral contraceptives were prescribed to relieve. If avoiding pregnancy is an issue, other forms of contraception can be considered.

MIGRAINE AND PREGNANCY

As many as 75% of women experience a decrease in the frequency of their migraine attacks during the last 6 months of pregnancy. Our experience suggests that migraine without aura (the most common type of migraine) is more likely to decrease during pregnancy than is migraine with aura, and that women with menstrual migraine are more likely to show a decrease in headache during pregnancy than are those without a clear menstrual association. The frequency of headaches may decrease as pregnancy progresses and estrogen levels stabilize at a high level. Many women get an increase in headaches during the first 3 months of pregnancy, sometimes before they even know they are pregnant. This can be a problem if they take medications that should not be taken during pregnancy.

We take a conservative position regarding the use of medication during pregnancy; we advise our patients to discontinue all medication prior to attempting to get pregnant. Preventive medications should be discontinued 2 to 4 weeks before attempting to conceive. Since medications that stop migraine acutely (such as the triptans or ergots) should not be used during pregnancy, the only safe time to use them if a patient is planning to conceive is during the first 10 days of the cycle after a true period. Medications that contain ergotamine (Cafergot) may cause uterine contraction and terminate a pregnancy. Insufficient information is available about the effect of the triptans on the uterus or the fetus to justify their use in pregnancy.

We prefer that patients do not smoke and use no caffeine, alcohol, or any medication during pregnancy, including any of the standard nonprescription off-the-shelf medications. However, when medication *must* be used during pregnancy, we urge our patients to fully discuss possible ramifications with their obstetrician and pediatrician. If medication is necessary, we recommend acetaminophen (Tylenol) over ASA, particularly during the first 3 months. If a more potent medication is required, opiates may be permitted for severe pain. When severe and protracted vomiting occurs, we suggest the use of an antinausea medication such as metoclopramide (Reglan) or ondansetron (Zofran). Steroids (dexamethasone or prednisone) can be prescribed for severe headache.

If attacks occur frequently and preventive medication is absolutely necessary, cyproheptadine (Periactin) has been rated by the US Food and Drug Administration as Category

B for use in pregnancy—"no evidence of risk in humans." Unfortunately it may not be that helpful. Some calcium channel blockers, β-blockers, and antidepressants can be used with caution. As with any other medications, use of preventive agents must be discussed thoroughly with your physicians.

POSTPARTUM PERIOD

After delivery, migraine may return with a vengeance, and quickly; in some women it may occur for the first time after delivery. Migraine and menstrual periods tend to be delayed in breastfeeding women because estrogen levels remain high as long as nursing continues. We prefer to avoid the use of medication in women who are breastfeeding. Refer to Table 16-2 for medications that should not be used when breastfeeding.

PERIMENOPAUSAL PERIOD

As women approach menopause, they may begin to notice subtle changes in the frequency, timing, duration, and amount of flow of their menstrual bleeding. Many women with preexisting migraine may notice that they get more headaches, perhaps due to fluctuating levels of estrogen and

Table 16-2 Medications Not To Be Used during Breastfeeding

Drug Generic Name	Brand Name
Ergotamine tartrate	Cafergot
Lithium	Lithotab
Amphetamine	Dexedrine
Chlorpromazine	Thorazine
ASA	Aspirin
Phenobarbital	—
Cyproheptadine	Periactin

progesterone. A small percentage of women may get their first migraines at this time—whether menopause occurs naturally or due to removal of the ovaries. If you are approaching menopause, be sure to mention your migraine history to your doctor; it may influence whether hormone replacement therapy (HRT) is implemented.

A large controversy has developed over the benefits and risks of HRT. The Women's Health Initiative Investigators reported in a major study in 2002 that combined HRT appeared to raise the risk of heart attack and stroke rather than lower it. The reasons for use of HRT have been reduced to control of hot flash–type symptoms and to treat osteoporosis.

If HRT is necessary, it should be given on a continuous basis rather than cyclically. If progesterone must be used (it helps to prevent cancer of the uterus if you have not had a hysterectomy), a low daily dose is preferable to a high dose taken 10 days per month.

If you notice that you get more frequent migraine after starting estrogen replacement therapy, you may find that a different estrogen preparation, especially one with a lower dose of estrogen, causes fewer headaches.

We recommend nonpharmacologic techniques of headache treatment during menopause (especially considering the new information about HRT), as well as vitamin supplements such as 400 international units of vitamin E. Recent studies have shown that the use of 400 mg of magnesium may be beneficial. We also suggest the use of 400 mg of vitamin B_2 (riboflavin) (see Chapter 12). Many off-the-shelf products are available that may decrease symptoms of low estrogen. Women have reported benefit from use of evening primrose oil, *Vitex* (chasteberry), and black cohosh, among other natural remedies.

CONCLUSION

Since women are more susceptible to migraine than are men, their unique needs require special consideration when migraine treatment plans are implemented. All hormonal issues need to be taken into account—menarche, menses, ovulation, pregnancy, and menopause. An interested physician will play a critical role in weaving these hormonal aspects into your care.

CHAPTER 17

TRAVEL, HOLIDAYS, AND HEADACHE

Although holidays are usually associated with good times, family reunions, and happy memories, they sometimes bring loneliness, depression, anxiety, and overcommitment—all of which can result in headache in those with the biologic vulnerability. Headache sufferers may also have more headaches when they travel, especially to high altitudes or damp rainy areas.

HOLIDAY HEADACHES

At The New England Center for Headache in Stamford, CT, we often receive up to three times more phone calls during the holiday season between Thanksgiving and New Year's Day than at most other times of year. We attribute this to the combined effects of stress factors and the greater exposure to headache triggers such as certain foods, partying in poorly ventilated and smoke-filled rooms, lack of sleep, and overcommitment (Figure 17-1).

Migraine patients are more affected than are others by changes in daily events and body rhythms, and the holidays magnify this susceptibility.

The following suggestions should be followed to avoid holiday headaches:

- Allow an unwinding period after your final day at work and before travel and celebration.
- Pace yourself realistically; try not to overextend yourself. Make a schedule that allows you to accomplish a reasonable number of tasks. Do not set unattainable goals.
- Be aware of signs of tension, such as clenched teeth, tense shoulders, and shallow breathing. When you note them, allow yourself a few moments to relax those muscles and take slow deep easy abdominal breaths.
- Try to sleep the same number of hours every night; try

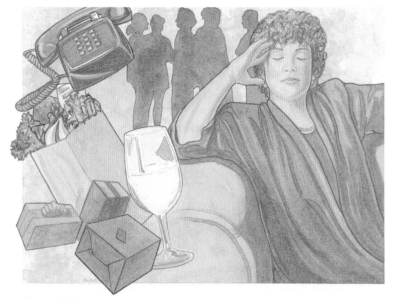

Figure 17-1 Holiday headaches are attributed to stress and exposure to such triggers as food, alcohol, parties, lack of sleep, and overcommitment.

going to bed at a set time and waking up at the same time. Set specific meal times; do not skip meals or even delay them. Exercise regularly most days of the week.

- Remember to take medications as prescribed; do not change dose times. Do not use more than recommended amounts of off-the-shelf or prescription pain medications.
- Take time to unwind after traveling or holiday activities; ease into your regular routine.

HANGOVER HEADACHE

The hangover headache is a familiar holiday phenomenon that is easier to avoid than to treat. Some tips on prevention follow:
- Drink very little alcohol and drink slowly, over a period of hours.

- The lighter-color alcohols such as gin, vodka, and white wine tend to have fewer congeners (impurities) and are less likely to cause hangover headache.
- Use sugar-free mixes to dilute the alcohol and make sure you drink sufficient nonalcoholic liquids.
- Drink approximately 355 mL (about 1^1/$_2$ cups) of plain water for every hour during which you consume alcohol.
- Before drinking, eat high-protein, more slowly absorbed foods, such as milk or mild cheese.
- High-fructose food such as apples, honey, grapes, tomatoes, and their juices may help you break down (metabolize) the alcohol faster.
- Stay in a well-ventilated room or go outdoors at intervals for fresh air; avoid inhaling cigarette smoke, which lowers the oxygen content of your blood and starves your brain for oxygen.
- Eat bland snacks, avoiding salt and foods that trigger your headaches.
- Go to bed at a reasonable hour and do not oversleep the next day.
- At bedtime take one or two tablets of ASA or off-the-shelf nonsteroidal anti-inflammatory drugs (NSAIDs) and drink as much water as possible. Put cold compresses over your forehead, eyes, temples, and/or the nape of your neck.
- Do not drink alcohol the next morning no matter how bad you feel.

AIR TRAVEL AND HEADACHE

Anxiety over or the stress of travel can trigger tension-type headache and migraine, as can cramped airplane seating conditions (Figure 17-2). Business- and first-class seating are generally more comfortable than is coach-class seating and

may be less likely to trigger a headache.

Headache may also occur because recirculated dry air with decreased oxygen content (or even cigarette smoke on some international flights) can stress your respiratory system, your brain, and your body's ability to regulate its temperature. Airplane cabins are pressurized to about 7,500 feet above sea level. This change affects many migraine sufferers; however, it affects cluster headache patients even more readily and flying may well produce a cluster attack, which is difficult to treat on a plane.

Traveling through time zones, especially toward the East, may cause jet lag; this, in turn, may bring on headaches for those who are sensitive to disruptions in their daily schedules of meals, sleep time, and waking time.

Figure 17-2 Travel hassles can trigger headache.

The time to start avoiding a travel headache is 24 hours before your flight! Leave plenty of time for all your activities, such as packing, getting to the airport, and checking in. If possible, check your bags and get your boarding pass at curbside check-in; this helps avoid muscle strain in your arms and neck due to carrying baggage any farther than necessary, moving your luggage frequently, and waiting in long lines. Try to get an aisle seat so you can get up and walk every 45 minutes or so. Move around while you wait for your flight—take little walks in the boarding area. While in flight do gentle neck exercises (as described on page 99) about once an hour.

If you are flying to Europe, you may be able to "reset" your body's biologic clock. Try to get a night flight and go to sleep when the plane takes off; request a blanket if you need one. (Blinders and earplugs may also help.) Your doctor may prescribe zolpidem (Ambien) or zaleplon (Sonata), which are relatively new short-acting sleeping pills, to help you get to sleep quickly and wake up refreshed. Melatonin is available off-the-shelf and may work for some people.

When your flight lands, try to adjust to the local time immediately: eat and sleep at the locally appropriate times and get a lot of morning daylight to help reset your brain's biologic clock to the new time zone. If you are flying west you should have less trouble, as long as you get to sleep early (which may be your own sleep time in the East).

Consider taking a headache medication, such as prescription Midrin or an off-the-shelf NSAID, before you leave for the airport and 3 hours later while you are on the plane when the flight attendant comes around with drinks. Or you can try taking a triptan at the gate before takeoff. Be sure to have headache medications with you in case you develop a severe headache in flight or in a foreign country. Keep medications in their original containers with proper labels and the name of your physician. Some countries may require that you have a letter from your doctor, particularly if you travel with opiates (narcotics) or injectable medications. In addition to medications you normally take for headache, your doctor may want you to have an opiate or steroid (dexamethasone [Decadron]) tablets on hand as backup treatment if your usual treatment does not work.

ALTITUDE HEADACHE

Even more than the temporary "altitude" of airplane cabin pressurization, high altitude in the mountains is a problem for certain migraineurs. If you spend considerable time at altitudes of 8,000 feet or higher, you may develop headaches whether you are biologically vulnerable or not.

Reduce your risk of altitude headache by avoiding alcohol, caffeine, and large amounts of pain medication. Be sure to drink sufficient fluids from the moment you arrive, pace yourself, do not overexert yourself, and take your headache medication as needed. For some patients acetazolamide (Diamox) 250 mg three times per day can prevent altitude headaches. Its major side effects include increased urination and tingling in the fingers and around the mouth. We sometimes prescribe dexamethasone (Decadron) 2 to 4 mg up to three times per day for a few days, beginning on the day patients arrive at high altitude; it is relatively safe if used for just a few days.

CONCLUSION

Holidays and travel are often fun, but they can be ruined by headaches. Proper treatment before and during these susceptible times can make a big difference in how you feel.

We truly hope that you have found this book useful in your search for relief and comfort. Doctors and researchers now can argue that we know as much about the underpinnings of migraine and related disorders as we do about other neurologic conditions such as epilepsy, Parkinson's disease, multiple sclerosis, and Alzheimer's disease. In fact, new data tell us that the burden of illness and prevalence of headache is greater than for all those diseases *combined!* The World Health Organization now lists the disability secondary to migraine in the top 20 list of worldwide disabling disorders.

The future is looking brighter for headache sufferers in terms of achieving the dream of control and prevention of headache, and being treated with credibility, understanding, and compassion. As the mysteries of the causes of migraine begin to unfold, and as new techniques in genetics, molecular biology, and functional imaging are improved, new targets are being identified for potential therapies. We think treatment and understanding of headache will change for the better in this first decade of the new millennium.

September 2002
The New England Center for Headache
Stamford, CT

INDEX

Page numbers ending in f represent figures; page numbers ending in t represent tables.